Travels in Place  *about a difficult and yet radiai* ... *ier's. The author leads us through* ... *becoming her mother's caregiver. S* ... *tise is not the helper she needs. Instead, humor, an open mind and a deep heart are the tools of the task before her. I guarantee you will laugh as much as you may cry, and you will learn much more than you ever knew about living from a woman whose daughter was walking with her to death. This is one book about the Alzheimer's journey that you won't be afraid to read.*

– Frena Gray-Davidson
Author of *The Alzheimer's Sourcebook* and
Alzheimer's FAQ

Christiane Griffin-Wehr, in relating her ever-changing experience with her mother's illness, has given us the combined gifts of information, compassion, and wisdom. She generously shares what she knows and learns about herself, her family, and her mother's increasingly serious condition of dementia. Her clarity and sense of humor and her sense of journeying with a loved one into unknown realms makes it obvious that there are events you can know and foresee, and things you can never expect to happen or fully understand. She encounters different kinds of medical care, some more helpful than others. This book goes a long way towards helping all of us who have aging parents to seek out living situations for them when necessary which will preserve their dignity and nurture body and soul as much as is humanly possible. This is a sad, funny, complex, and very wise book.

– Jane Pincus
Co-author of *Our Bodies, Ourselves*
Co-Founder of *Our Bodies Ourselves* (OBOS),
also known as the Boston Women's Health Book
Collective (BWHBC), a nonprofit, public interest
women's health education, advocacy,
and consulting organization.

TRAVELS IN PLACE

A Journey into Memory Loss

Christiane W. Griffin-Wehr

Robert D. Reed Publishers   ●   Bandon, OR

Robert D. Reed Publishers
P.O. Box 1992
Bandon, OR 97411
Phone: 541-347-9882; Fax: -9883
E-mail: 4bobreed@msn.com
Website: www.rdrpublishers.com

Editors: Cynthia Duncan, Paul Wehr, and Cleone Lyvonne
Cover Designer: Cleone Lyvonne
Cover Photo: Ilse G. Wängler with her father, ca. 1928, from author's private collection
Interior Designers: Jan Moore and Amy Cole
Inside Photos: From author's private collection

ISBN: 978-1-934759-10-3
ISBN 10: 1-934759-10-4
Library of Congress Number: 2008925456

Manufactured, Typeset, and Printed in the
United States of America.

Dedication

In honor of

My Beloved Mom,
for giving me the extraordinary privilege of this Life,
and

Dear Curtis and Paul,
for making its living so meaningful and
eminently pleasurable

Acknowledgments

When someone asked me recently how long I'd been working on this book, I was stunned to hear myself answer that it has been almost ten years since I recorded my first notes on this journey. I was not surprised, however, to recall the long list of people who provided immeasurable support throughout this decade of work:

- Emily and the counselors at Boulder County Aging Services, whose kindness and professional expertise kept me from falling into the crack that split my world with Mom's illness.
- My colleagues at the University of Colorado, whose understanding and flexibility enabled me to be both caregiver and professional.
- The staff at Juniper Village at Wellspring, Louisville, who cared for Mom and loved her better than we could have done alone.
- Running buddies Annie, Judith, and Mary, who encouraged my stories every step of the way.
- Good friend and extraordinary grammar-policewoman Cynthia who, as unflinching draft-reader, believed in this project from the start.
- Ron, Jen, Jane, Jim, Linda, Horace, Gordon, Lois, Gladi, and all of Mom's family and friends, who remembered her throughout her illness and gathered after her death to allow her spirit to host one more celebration of life.

- Bob, Cleone, and Amy, the marvelous Robert D. Reed Publishers team who took a chance by accepting my typescript for publication and worked skillfully and cheerfully to make it as good as it could be.
- My sister, Ute, whose partnership made the load bearable and whose willing listening assured that every one of those hundreds of cell-phone minutes was well-spent.
- My son, Curtis, who, while losing his own dear Omi, remained ever-helpful to his Mom and wise beyond his years.
- My husband, Paul, whose faithful constancy and patient love guided me through seemingly endless rewrites of not only this text, but of my life. He is both the solid ground I walk on and the wings that give me flight.

Thank you all!

Foreword

One of the mixed blessings of modern medicine is that increasingly we have the capacity to outlive our minds. Unfortunately, our ingenuity can outrun our bodies in the aging race. The result can be frightful forgetfulness with the accompanying ache of loneliness that we label dementia. For victims, as well as their family, friends, and caregivers, this is a painful pilgrimage into scary and uncharted territory.

I once had a friend who, upon learning that he had incurable cancer, asked me to walk the final journey with him. While I could never deny such a request, I had to warn him that I had not traveled this road before. "Neither have I," he responded. "We'll just have to figure it out together as we go." We did, and the experience for me was deeply instructive and profoundly life changing.

Christiane Griffin-Wehr, in **Travels in Place**, invites us to accompany her and her mom on such a journey. As she grasps her mother's hand and walks with her through the darkening eclipse of dementia, she forges a path into the unknown with an unwavering commitment dictated by a promise to always be there for her "dear Mom."

Though set in the context of the debilitating effects of dementia, this book becomes a celebration of the healing power of love. While being dragged into the depths of the pain of separation over which she has no control, Chris discovers one of life's eternal truths—that unconditional love can transcend even the fearsome threat of memory loss and separation and can offer peace, healing, and completeness in the darkest night of the soul.

Of all the books that line my study shelves, there are only

a few to which I return again and again. Those have two things in common. Each in its own way addresses the human condition with a sensitivity and authenticity that rings true to my life experience. And each offers the gift of redemptive insights that can come only from walking through the valley of life's deepest shadows. *Travels in Place* is the latest addition to that special collection of writings that I cherish and will read and reread. And I assure you, that if you accept the invitation to walk this road with Chris and her "dear Mom," you too will come to cherish the gift they offer.

– The Rev. Gordon Ward, Retired
Lutheran Campus Ministry Chaplain
University of Michigan, Ann Arbor and
University of Colorado Boulder
February 14, 2008

Table of Contents

Introduction

The highest object that human beings can set before themselves is not the pursuit of any such chimera as the annihilation of the unknown; it is simply the unwearied endeavor to remove its boundaries a little further from our own little sphere of action.
—Thomas H. Huxley (1825 - 1895)

I WAS NOT yet three years old when men[1] first reached the summit of Mount Everest. Where others had tried and many died, on May 29, 1953, two mountaineers walked steadfastly up and into that ever-present plume flagging Everest's peak to lift the veil of mystery from those heights for the first time. Getting to the top, and safely back down, was lauded as a superhuman accomplishment, something long assumed unwise at best, and deadly at worst. And for a war-weary world, news of this feat did much more than celebrate the conquest of Earth's highest mountain. The successful ascent signaled to the world's Western human consciousness that another step had been taken toward proving Huxley wrong! Clearly, given sufficient skill, stamina, and a reasonable measure of God's own good luck, "annihilation of the unknown" does not have to be an illusion: perhaps we *can* push the boundaries of human limitation far enough to vanquish the indecipherable darkness and blinding light surrounding us. And so we still dare to believe.

I was not precocious enough at age three to be aware of either the conquest of Everest or its furthering humanity's

---

1   And so they were. The first woman, Junko Tabei from Japan, would reach the summit of Everest 22 years later, on May 16, 1975.

1

belief in its boundless abilities. But certainly by then, while clutching the hand of Opa Vagt, my beloved maternal grandfather, I had begun to cherish our wonder-filled explorations of the woods surrounding our home in northern Germany. Granted, by Himalayan standards, Nature's expression in the Sachsenwald is as tame as an English country garden. But to a child (*this* child anyway), the dense shadowy forests were quite dark and forbidding enough to encourage my imagining wild and wonderful things. This inclination had already been finely tuned in a home my parents had endowed with far more books, musical scores and artwork than its walls or shelf-space could neatly accommodate. I was thus introduced early in life to both the mystical power of Nature and a genre of literature that often offered at least a partial explanation of its magic.

Little wonder, then, that the first book I recall subjecting to the dog-earing and underlining abuse that came to mark my reading and re-reading favorite passages was a German children's *Reader's Digest* with an account of Sir Edmund Hillary's and Tenzing Norgay's historic journey to the top of Mount Everest. Its maps, charts and photographs persuaded me then and there that I too wanted to participate in this human experience that's capable of finding a way safely through the exhausting, often terrifying, but always exciting and eminently satisfying geography of life.

Here I am on an expedition in the woods of northern Germany, ca. 1955.

As I grew, so did my collection of adventure books. My attention moved across continents and countries, and I practiced speaking exotic words until Kilimanjaro and Ngorongoro rolled easily off my tongue. The creation of Tanzania's Serengeti National Park fueled my imagination, as did ocean voyages and scientific endeavors, dog-sled treks, and jungle adventures. I was enthralled by descriptions of human exposure to Nature raw and unrefined, always followed by the reassurance that human potential and endurance can prevail against formidable odds. I never tired of reading how those who were not deterred by the unknown could live in or travel through inhospitable regions, because they knew to draw on a vast reservoir of human adaptability, cooperation, and ingenuity. With uncertainty a constant companion, they braved the extremes of uncharted realms. In doing so, they challenged their readers to resurrect for themselves that tolerance for the unpredictable that seems to have atrophied in those of us who have forsaken the journey of life, preferring instead to treat it like a trip—planned, prepaid, and insured.

Despite my early adventuring with my grandfather, and my childhood fascination with the challenge of the unknown lifted from the printed page, the years transformed me. As happens to most of us, somewhere along the way I, too, had grown into an adult seeking comfort and familiarity in my travels. Preferring my trips orderly and predictable, I engaged in open-ended journeying only reluctantly. However, by the time I turned fifty, the undeniable symptoms of my mother's evolving memory loss forced me to undertake what felt overwhelmingly like an out-of-control venture. And I returned, for new insights perhaps, to my childhood source of comfort by reading the accounts of explorers who knew what it meant to forge on even while endlessly stuck in place or steadily losing ground.

I hadn't left home, mind you, but I was growing desperate to learn how to survive the wasteland of Mom's advancing dementia. I found myself looking for ever more extreme examples of the human capacity to endure discomfort, disappointment, and the sense of being hopelessly adrift that surely explorers like Shackleton, Nansen, and Scott must have felt. While modern medicine could give me a broad frame of reference for my journey, it was in the diaries of those who had lived days, weeks, and months of mind-numbing darkness, constant uncertainty, and unutterable loneliness that I found a kinship of experience. That was sufficient to keep me searching for recognizable features in the uncharted territory of Mom's mind—

3

some guidance for how to reach the next knoll, or island, or rock-outcropping in order to gain, if not sound sleep, at least some rest.

I've found no signs directing me safely through the precarious footing of walking with a loved one through a demented world, and I offer no roadmap. Hell, there is no road! But I have stumbled far enough along the path to recognize that, the unceasing human effort to know notwithstanding, Huxley was in fact right. We will not soon, or perhaps ever, eliminate the Unknown from human experience. Indeed, doing so may not even be humanity's purpose on Earth.

Instead, I've learned that we are here simply to bring a candle's flicker into the fearsome darkness of memory loss and a warm touch to the icy loneliness of the forgetting. Certainly I needed the reassurance of scientific fact as much as the next person. But having been taught as a child that darkness is nothing to fear—it's just the sun lighting the other side of the earth after all—brought me cold comfort when walks through the woods with my grandfather lasted into the darkening evening. What made me feel safe was the warm strength of his hand around mine!

The recognition that human fellowship and understanding along the way may well prove more valuable than logical explanations held true for me as I was searching for landmarks of hope, love, and fulfillment in the barren landscape of the mind of someone afflicted with dementia. As true as it did for Cherry-Garrard when he concluded his riveting account of Antarctic exploration in *The Worst Journey in the World*[2] with:

"... some will tell you that you are mad. And nearly all will say, 'What is the use?' ...And so you will sledge nearly alone, but those with whom you sledge will not be shopkeepers. And that is worth a good deal. If you march your Winter Journeys you shall have your reward, so long as all you are after is a penguin's egg."

---

2   Cherry-Garrard, Apsley, *The Worst Journey in the World,* National Geographic Adventure Classic, 1922, p. 557.

Perhaps you, too, have taken up the caregiver's harness. And though I don't know what strength and stories you bring to hauling that heavy load of your loved one's vacant eyes, I can see you as clearly as the men on polar sledging treks I saw in those grainy, early photographs. Hooded heads bent low into the storm, shoulders leaning hard into the weight they are dragging, and feet unsteady on the treacherous ice. You are doing no less. Whatever your burden, I thank you fellow sledgers for pulling along with me. And for knowing that it is all worth it when through the veil of unrecognizing eyes shines an occasional glimmer of connection with you, past or present.

Starting at the Beginning

There is no easy way into another world.
—James Salter, *Solo Faces*

TWO WRITERS IN the naturalist/adventure genre that comprised so much of my reading became favorites early on and have yet to be displaced. One is the Canadian author Farley Mowat. His unparalleled skill at combining empathy for the plight of our Earth and her creatures with rich humor permits Mowat to make the reader listen to and understand the most dire and complex

My beloved maternal grandfather, Opa Vagt, and I, ca. 1952

situations. As a storyteller of non-fiction with few peers, he has caused more than an occasional puzzled glance to come my way as I laughed out loud when reading his work in public places.

The second is the naturalist Peter Matthiessen. His *The Snow Leopard* blends journaling of heart and geography seamlessly. Prolifically producing works of fiction and nonfiction, Matthiessen was once asked, during a lecture at the University of Colorado years ago, in which of the genres he prefers to write. Refusing labels, he shared his conviction that he really doesn't see a difference between the two. If you can imagine, believe, or write it, he went on to explain, chances are someone somewhere has lived it. With that observation I felt myself and my story explained. For while appreciating the well-spun novel, I'm generally more interested in biographies and histories; they remind me that truth *is* stranger than fiction and validate my own life course as proof of that assertion.

There is one drawback though. While true stories may be more interesting, where does one start the telling? If this memoir were all the work of imagination, I could simply choose a moment and place and go from there. Maybe that's one attraction to writing fiction. I, however, was trying to recount the sequence of events in the *real* lives my Mom and I shared. And beginning that effort, I felt as overwhelmed as I did the day I was later asked by a writer to talk about my care-giving role for an article she was writing.

When *did* it begin? I had no idea what to tell the expectant face sitting across from me. In sixty minutes, the interviewer was looking for material for a neat, two-page article on the experiences of adult children caring for their aging parents. Whether determined by circumstance or choice, as a fifty-something daughter caring daily for her seventy-something mother, I did qualify for sharing my story. Beyond that, the telling got a little complicated.

Her opening question was straightforward enough: "Have you always been close to your mom?"

"Oh, no!" The words spilled out of my mouth before I realized how much easier it would have been to take the hook and just say, "Yes." But I was supposed to be telling it like it was. And it was, well, a bit more involved than that. "Actually no, my favorite parent, hands down, was my father. My favorite live-in adult was my maternal grandfather, whom I adored. Then there was my dad's sister, dear Tante Käthe, or my godparents from Zürich... no, Mom was great to have around, but my favorite? She didn't even make the first cut. She was my Mom."

To gather some wind back into her sails, my interviewer skillfully took a different mental tack: "So when or how did you become your Mom's main caregiver?"

Ouch, here we go. "Well in some ways I started *taking*

care of Mom long before her illness. I'd always been Mom's interpreter, translating the intricacies of both the English language and American culture for her."

"I see." We both politely pretended not to notice that she obviously didn't: "So the U.S. isn't your mom's native country?"

Here we go, I thought, as my heart went out to the poor woman trying to stay on task while she pieced together the story of Mom's and my relationship. I forged bravely ahead: "No, we were all from Germany. My family didn't move to the U.S. until I was thirteen. Mom and I wanted to remain at Home (that is, Germany), while my sister cherished the thrilling newness of 'Amerika.' But most important, Dad had been offered a tenured position at the University of Colorado. It was an honor he couldn't refuse, and so," I finished, smiling, "here we are."

"Oh, okay." Her words strained for clarity her eyes did not reflect. Still, maybe we could stay on track: "Then your mom and you were united in your desire to stay in Germany?"

"Yes, definitely that." Maybe I could just leave it at that? It was tempting. "But," I heard myself continue, "being united in our sadness and confusion with having to leave our beloved homeland didn't bring us closer at first. In fact, I went out of my way to make Mom's life difficult as I struggled with a high school culture I neither liked nor understood. By my senior year, I was carrying the child of the school's only African American star athlete. You can imagine that an eighteen-year-old bearing a biracial child in the U.S. in 1969 was not that common or readily accepted. But my parents, especially my Mom, stood by me to support and guide what would turn out to be one of the best decisions I ever made, to keep and raise my son."

"Ahh... " the relief in the interviewer's voice was audible as she reached for the same handle we all remember from Psychology 101. She barely concealed her triumph: " ...you feel you *owe* your Mom."

Finally the story was taking shape in her mind, at least for a moment. "No, not at all. If there was anything I felt I needed to repay, that debt was more than settled when Mom moved back in with Curtis and me after Dad left."

Not defeated, but nearing exasperation, my interviewer switched tactics yet again. No longer willing to jump to conclusions, she merely repeated: "So your dad left your mom?"

"Yes, about fifteen years after giving up everything loved and familiar to follow her husband to the USA, Mom was alone here. Dad returned to Germany with his new wife, a student more than thirty years his junior."

Her final "Oh" was followed by a long silence. Apparently she couldn't muster the courage to ask about what else I might drag up.

Who could blame her? Except that I really wasn't trying to be obtuse. Cute didn't work for me as a teenager, and I sure wasn't going to settle for it now that life felt serious indeed. Given the constraints of her task, I felt enough empathy with her to skip rather superficially through the remaining minutes of the interview. But any notions of discovering the rules of Cartesian logic in our tale are best abandoned now. Neither our life stories, nor Mom's dementia, lend themselves to the artificial neatness of "if-then" sequences. The defining truths of life are invariably more complex than that, aren't they?

My care-giving role, stranger than fiction, remember, is that while we had never been particularly good *friends* or even had the kind of emotional closeness that allows you to share your innermost secrets, my mother and I had also never lived entirely independent of one another—or wanted to. Neither of us had a history of being clingy, unopinionated, nor incapable—quite the opposite was true. Still, Mom's life and mine had been somehow inseparably intertwined by far more than the physical bond birth forges between mother and child. If we were tied neither by knots, nor by unchallenged agreement with or blind acceptance of the other, it was partly mutual need that held our lives together, to be sure. But above all, what bound us so closely was that Mom and I had always shared an inherent mutual understanding of what matters most to us in life at which moment. That, I suppose, had begun with my birth.

Home Base: 1950-1999

*Our job is not to change people
so God can accept them, our job is to accept people
so God can change them.*
—John Nunes

My older sister Ute was born in 1945. She and I had little in common; five years and vastly different interests separated the two Wängler girls for decades. For ringing so true, I took solace in Homer J. Hickam Jr.'s response (*October Sky*, Island Books, Dell Publishing, 1998, p. 21) to being asked whether he was an only child. "Yes," he quipped, "and so was my brother." Happily, in Mom's illness, Ute and I found a shared goal and purpose for her well-being that has transformed our relationship into an appreciative, loving friendship.

AT THE AGE of twenty-seven, late in 1950, Mom gave birth to her second daughter in Hamburg, Germany. Life was still spare. Mom had been forced to give up her career as a professional violinist in Hamburg's distinguished city orchestra to focus on helping her husband and their first child survive the physical ruins and emotional rubble that was postwar Germany. But by 1949, with my Dad a promising PhD student, my parents felt secure enough to consider enlarging the family. The stifling fog of loss and shortages was beginning to lift, and the remarkable resilience of the human spirit that seeks life in even the darkest times was clearly visible in pregnant young women everywhere. Soon my mother, carrying me beneath her heart with joyous anticipation, was among them. As

11

a result, my earliest recollections are of a pervasive sense that parents, grandparents, my whole world took pleasure in my arrival; even my cousins contributed by declaring it just perfect to have a new baby born in November. What they meant was that now an annual birthday gathering would brighten what is arguably the grayest, dreariest month in northern Germany. Little wonder I felt welcomed and wanted.

A claim of a happy childhood, I'm well aware, is suspect these days. At best it is viewed as the imagining of a slightly deluded mind. At worst it's blamed on total denial. Besides, whatever else may be their eventual effects, happy childhoods do not make for interesting stories. Psychotherapists earn a good living repairing the damage, while much artistic expression thrives on veiled references to having been misunderstood and mistreated as a child. Frank McCort is more direct. On the first page of his memoir, *Angela's Ashes*,[3] he comes right out and asserts: "It (childhood) was, of course, miserable: the happy childhood is hardly worth your while." Well, I disagree and can't relate to such an assertion, even when spoken by the humorously defensive tongue of a survivor. I can only say that I genuinely remember mine as a healthy upbringing: one I believe provided me with something richly valuable not only during those precarious early years, but far beyond. Thus my relationship with Mom resulted neither from an ill-conceived union nor neglectful, unwise parenting. I can't even conjure up a decent dose of repressed guilt or expressed anger. And if I occasionally envy great writers the romance of a childhood lost, I cannot claim it. I grew up, and largely remain, loved, loving, and unapologetically happy.

That is not to say that I did not experience the interesting people or difficult events that help us mature. Sibling rivalry and bike wrecks (one involving hospitalization for a fairly serious head wound) were standard fare in my young life. From adults' conversations overheard as murmurings in my bed, I'd occasionally catch horrifying bits about the unimaginable suffering inflicted and endured during "The War," so recently ended. But I learned quickly to silence them

---

3   McCort, Frank, *Angela's Ashes,* Touchstone Press, 1996, p. 11

by putting the pillow over my head, and I prefer to go to sleep that way to this day. Then, of course, there were my occasional trips to the school principal's office. My parents would punish these with, for me, the worst of all options: I would have to take the train to school rather than joining my three friends in our usual, fast, freewheeling bike ride through the twelve wooded miles separating our town from our school.

I have vague recollections of a drunken uncle taking a dive off the porch into the rose bushes one New Year's Eve (with no lasting ill effect to either him or the plants). And I remember an exceptionally fierce North Sea storm, drowning several of the islands off the coast, and driving the Elbe River, long tamed by shipping-locks, into such a threatening frenzy that my dad did something previously unheard of in my life. To get us home safely, he picked my friends and me up from school in our car! But on the whole, no hardships invaded the first thirteen years of my life that couldn't be fixed by a visit to my grandfather's room where his mischievous eyes, a private stash of licorice, and offers of a walk through the woods were ever-present balm for such unhappy occasions. Self-involved as I was, and courting my friends and favorite adults, Mom hardly figured in my life. She was just one part of a harmonious whole.

ALL THAT CHANGED forever in June of 1964 as the Norwegian freighter, Havlom, slid slowly westward through the English Channel. She carried our forlorn little family of four, as well as our VW station wagon, most of our furniture and eight other passengers, past the White Cliffs of Dover and away from all we ever knew and loved. Confined to Havlom's broad decks, we moved inexorably closer to an unknown future. America.

While my dad and sister Ute waxed poetic about all that lay ahead, Mom and I clung to stories of what we were leaving behind. Perhaps as a bridge to the steadily receding past, our lives as we'd known them, we spent much of

I was five when Mom's mother died and her father, my Opa Vagt, happily for me, moved into a room in the large, rambling upstairs of a lovely old home my parents rented in Aumühle about an hour outside Hamburg in the Sachsenwald.

the ten-day crossing looking back. We reminisced especially about my maternal grandmother—the one for whom Mom would later endlessly search in her illness. I know little of Mom's "Mum" from personal experience. But I do remember oft-repeated tales of her internal strength and sense of purpose. All that she did was focused relentlessly on the goal of protecting those she loved at all costs. In the late nineteenth century, her mother had raised her thirteen children against formidable odds. As the keeper of a frequently absent, wealthy sea captain's wine cellar, my great-grandfather had become a pathological alcoholic—a mean one.

I was told that every Friday evening saw a race as my great-grandmother, with determined face, marched from bar to bar in search of her husband and enough of his paycheck to cobble together a meal for her children. If he eluded her, he'd not only drink away his earnings but gleefully feed the tasty leftovers from his *Gasthaus* visits to the cats before his hungry children's eyes. Fortunately, she didn't fail often and thus successfully raised her brood, my grandmother among them, with a loathing of alcohol and an uncompromising, no-nonsense approach to doing what's right and fair.

Two world wars provided my grandmother ample opportunity to show her own loyalties and compassion. One of my favorite mental images is of my mother with my grandmother resolutely (and courageously) refusing to bow to Nazi uniforms and rifles as they staged their menacing presence in Hamburg. Her head held high, with her somewhat scared but hugely impressed (as I heard Mom tell it!) daughter firmly by the hand, my Oma Vagt would march straight past the Brownshirts and their malevolently smeared warnings on her butcher's shop window, "JEW—Don't shop here." The proprietor was

14

her friend. Despite my grandparents' poverty, he had given her a fair deal and the best cuts of meat for years. No one would now convince or force her to shop elsewhere. I understood Mom's anguished longing for her mother; we did need that woman in our lives!

Or, maybe we had her with us all along? With the non-negotiable exception of siding with her beloved husband whether he was right or wrong, Mom was not prone to delusions. She was fiercely pragmatic and rigorously honest, especially with herself. And if, at least initially, it didn't foster friendship between us, Mom's iron will in supporting Dad's dream, which took us into that alien world of America, wasn't lost on me. As did generations of proud women before her, Mom traveled the miles between those worlds with so much grace that we barely noticed how distressing it was for her.

I remember seeing her resolve crack only once. We had spent four days on the highways carrying us from New York harbor toward our destination out west. Although we had never seen the land where we were headed, we were buoyed by the information we'd been given by Americans who had been to the Swiss Alps that our destination, Boulder, Colorado, was known as the "Switzerland of America." The narrow gauge railroad of the early twentieth century running just west of what would be our new home was even known as the "Switzerland Trail." To be sure, Mom appreciated the genuine. She was not an ersatz sort of person, and such comparisons were never wholly reassuring. But the promise of anything familiar, especially something resembling the beautiful surroundings evoking happy memories of times in Zürich and Bern, must have helped ease her mind.

So we gamely continued westward hopefully scanning the horizon. But there's no denying that our optimism had waned by the time we'd put that long succession of vowel-states, Ohio, Indiana, Illinois, and Iowa, behind us. We had been moving across the continent for miles now, hundreds of miles. And as we moved farther west, the expanse of flat, dry prairie stretching out before us made it harder and harder to believe the voices that had been sustaining our flagging spirits: "Colora-

15

do. Oh yes, it's beautiful there! Just like Switzerland." As the pages turned on our AAA mileage map, the mood change in the car became palpable and our suspicions grew from faint disbelief to pure incredulity. The miles of western Nebraska and eastern Colorado—*Colorado*, we'd been told, the *Switzerland of America* after all—were not revealing anything remotely resembling the lush meadows, brown dairy cows, and snow-covered peaks I remembered from visits with my godparents at the Zürichsee. This region we now traveled, parched by the sun and buffeted by relentless winds, would not, even by the farthest stretch of my willing imagination, be transformed over the next two hundred miles to Boulder into anything remotely like any part of Switzerland I'd ever seen. Not a chance in hell.

I was mostly amused and a little curious whether those who had suggested this resemblance were deluded or simply blind. But for Mom the claim of that resemblance was a matter of survival. And though she had already put behind her heart-wrenching goodbyes and the endless gray waves of the Atlantic to support her husband's move to this unfamiliar country, it wasn't until we huddled in the spare shade of a group of cottonwoods to escape the noontime Colorado sun for our picnic lunch that I saw my mother cry for the first time in my memory. She silently wept desperate tears, offering only a glimpse of the well of sadness hidden underneath.

As we continued westward, we did, of course, see that immense wall of mountains emerge on the horizon just a few hours later. Knowing our journey would end just short of that enormous obstacle, I'm sure we greeted the vision with far more pleasure and relief than the pioneers on those early wagon trains must have felt. For us, even while searching for Switzerland, the mountains were awe-inspiring. And in their beauty the Rocky Mountains brought, if not an end to all of Mom's tears, at least reinforcement to her resolve. With her family around her, she knew she was getting closer to home.

MY OWN ADJUSTMENTS to our new home were not as graceful as were Mom's. When school started two months after our
June arrival, I didn't easily make the switch from Germany
where I had been a tomboy adept at ruling my home turf to
Boulder where I felt as foreign as everyone assumed me to be.
Trying to fit into the hormone-charged insecurities of life in
an American junior high school, I was handicapped further by
my classical education at a German *Gymnasium*. I had been
taught several years of Latin and French, but had received
less than a year of textbook English instruction. That proved
woefully inadequate for fitting in, though what really upset my
sense of self was the fact that I had suddenly lost my name.

I began life as Christiane Wängler. My parents' selec-
tion of "Christian," a common, melodic German name, had had
the added advantage of needing only a feminine vowel ending
should their second child be another girl. And so *Christiane*
(chris-tie-áh-né) it was. But four syllables, with no middle
name to fall back on, immediately proved too cumbersome for
five-year-old sister Ute. She casually dropped the first two syllables, renaming me for herself and the world "*Jani*" (Yah-nie).
Her creation served me well for thirteen years of my life.

But childhood sooner or later ends for us all, and mine
ended abruptly that September in Boulder as I started ninth
grade at Southern Hills Junior High School. I would never
walk holding the hand of my beloved grandfather again. I'd
never return to the woods or feed sugar cubes to the horses at
the riding stables near our home. And it would be a long, long
time before I would move again as freely and securely as Jani
did, even while tripping over their umbrellas as she and her
boisterous friends would race frantically from school trying to
catch the first train home.

If giving up our extended family, friends, and sense of
place in Germany caused me temporarily to lose my bearings,
it was losing my name that robbed me of my sense of who I
was. The English alphabet has no single-letter equivalents
to the German umlaut vowel's combination whereby the pro-
nunciation of a, o, and u becomes ä, ö, and ü. In English the
umlaut vowels are created with the insertion of an "e" immedi-

17

ately following the affected letter, thereby noting the distinction between an 'a' and an 'ä.' Thus, my family name Wängler legally became Waengler. And in the United States, my sister wasn't the only one who struggled with my first name. Every embarrassed teacher's stammering during roll call—"uh, Kristy...uhm...Anne?"—quickly persuaded me to accept the pragmatic solution everyone suggested and drop that really not very important *a*. Little did the whole class know turning to look at the new girl, Christine Waengler, that I was searching for her at least as hard as they were.

At that point, however, my happy childhood sense of security served me well. The whole notion of *being lost,* as a relative concept, is something that had never bothered me much. Lostness, after all, is only relevant in relation to something else—a different plan, another destination, an unfulfilled idea. As Mark Twain said: "You're not lost if you don't care where you are." So if one doesn't expect to be somewhere else, one isn't lost—right? And if I could do one thing well, it was adapt to my surroundings and make them my own. As professional musicians, my parents noting my ability to repeat quickly and exactly what I'd heard would proudly say: "Jani has an excellent ear!" Using slightly different words, I'd agree more lightly, "Yup, I would have made a great parrot."

Call it what you will, it is true that during our regular vacations to southern Germany, I was the one called upon to translate the guttural *Süd-Deutsch* of the locals. Even with his head firmly tucked into the belly of the cow he was milking, and his words squarely addressing the swollen udder, I could easily understand the farmer's four a.m. mumblings. I had no trouble deciphering the language of the realm whether his directions were intended for me, the cow, or the nearby cats awaiting their share of the rich, warm liquid. At the end of our visit Mom could discard my pants, too soiled and scented with muck for more gentrified northern Germany; but the southern German accent I'd unwittingly perfected in just two or three weeks there stayed with me long after our return home. Blending in with such ease and grasping language quickly may not have helped Jani find Christine Waengler in Colorado. But it assured that others could. And I saw to it that they would!

As the self-appointed commander-in-chief, I deliberately set about my transformation. If I was going to have to function as a modern American teenage girl, rather than the German small-town roughneck I had been just eight weeks before, so be it. I switched roles with the precision of a "take-no-prisoners" operation, and heedless of my own or anyone else's sensibilities, lived the changes ruthlessly, totally, and perhaps most damaging, abruptly. Powerless to reclaim what we'd left behind, I wasn't about to waste time grieving for Jani, or Home, or any of it, and instead resorted to doing the one thing I knew reliably how to do: adapt to fit in.

Besides, who better than a teenager, when Nature's design already urges mind and body to give up childish ways, gets the opportunity for such a complete and legitimate remake? It took only one disapproving look from my new peers for me to realize that a bicycle, the vehicle epitomizing freedom and independence just a few months ago, would not do in this new world. Exposure to sun, wind, and rain were no longer assets to the ride, but instead destroyed my carefully crafted hair-do, threatened to tear the nylons that had replaced my cotton socks, and smudged the make-up I'd carefully applied to my eyes. Most important, the boys, no longer good buddies wildly pedaling next to me but now potential *boyfriends*, were all riding the bus.

For it was, of course, all about the boys. In little more than a year after our arrival, I, too, was "going steady"—and my boyfriend was a coup. He was our high school's tall, very dark, and very handsome star athlete. A recent transplant from a New Jersey ghetto, this young African American man was trying to recreate himself at least as hard as I was. Reinvention was something that, in the end, American society permitted him to do far less successfully than I could. But that didn't stop us from trying. Together we explored our new identities as we pushed societal norms as far as possible during our early high school years. Of course, we experimented with physical maturity. So even though it should not have surprised anyone, least of all me, everyone seemed genuinely shocked to realize that, pregnant late in my senior year of high school, I'd be

19

acquiring yet another name. *Mom*, to Curtis Monroe Griffin, remains the enduring name and identity I'll proudly wear to my dying day.

Though Curtis's father and I were willing partners and parents, our eighteen-year old flesh and minds proved weak. Lacking maturity to cope with the complexities of the life we'd created for ourselves, our marriage deteriorated into frustration, faithlessness, and violence. What never wavered for a moment was my delighted devotion to the child who made me "Mom." I was utterly besotted with my beautiful, smiling son.

John Thomas Griffin and I had a son, Curtis Monroe Griffin, born June 26, 1969.

Thankfully, that love did not render me senseless. Even in my clearly befuddled state, I heard the gravity of the messages about *being black* in 1960s America. Whatever else was true about the choices Curtis's father and I had made, by creating a biracial person, we had ensured another layer of complexity for Curtis's young life, that added to the difficulties our youth, lack of education, and insufficient financial means had already placed there. Our utter lack of preparedness for the task of raising a child responsibly made it obvious very quickly that if we were not to disadvantage Curtis further, John and I needed to grow up apart from one another.

When Curtis was barely one year old, his dad and I separated and he and I moved into my parents' home where Curtis blossomed under my mother's protective, pragmatic love. I, too, was restored. The name Christiane, inconvenient though attention to that pesky little *a* might have been, was restored to all of my documents of record. So was the W. of my maiden name. Griffin, being my legal bond to my son, came last. Finally, with my name accurately reflecting my life experiences to that point by honoring both my roots and branches, I settled into being addressed mostly as Mom. Friends continued to call me Chris, but officially

I was finally who I felt myself to be: Christiane W. Griffin.

I know it would be much tidier if I could say that I am still the person with that name. But life is not stagnant, and this is not the end of the story. If anything convinces me of our ability to travel, richly rewarded in Place, then it must be that after thirty years in the same community I underwent yet another transformation. In August 1999, I married again. Uniting my own, Curtis's and my husband's names, Jani Wängler has grown to become: Christiane W. Griffin-Wehr. But that's getting ahead of the story.

MAYBE THESE DAYS it's not as rare for fledglings in their twenties to return to the parental nest after university studies or other worldly pursuits. But in the 1970s, it was unusual for parents to put out the welcome mat for an unwed mother (don't hear so much of unwed fathers of whom, logic would seem to dictate, there must be at least as many?) with a biracial son in tow. In fact, admonitions against my decision as a single, white mother to raise my son were numerous. Much advice came from well-meaning experts in social services and family relations who agreed that if we truly loved Curtis we'd make him available for adoption by an African American couple. They would not only really want him, but, sharing the same racial attributes, would actually be able to better understand and relate to my son than I ever could.

Wise though such advice may have been, and without disparaging the noble and necessary work of adoptive families, when it came time for my parents to live their conviction, they never wavered. They were not dissuaded from their belief that given the availability of basic resources, including love and finances (we had plenty of the former, and enough of the latter), no one can better care for a child than the immediate, biological family. Besides, wasn't Curtis just as much the fifty percent German that our side of this family had thrown into his genes regardless of assumptions others would make based on the warm, sun-kissed café-au-lait color of his skin?

Looking back on it, my decision could just as easily have spelled ruin. That it didn't—Mom, Dad, Curtis and I all thrived under this new family configuration—is in no small part due to Curtis's light, conciliatory approach to life. Evident the first time I laid eyes on him, that openness remains the core of his successful survival today. Curtis's nature blended beautifully with the fabric of our cooler northern European temperament to create something richer and warmer among us.

The linchpin, though, was Mom. I spent my days earning a technical degree as a veterinary technician and working in an animal hospital. Dad toodled the few miles to his office at the university on his new Vespa, and Mom and Curtis developed a bond forged of love and steel. Curtis did more to define home and family for Mom here in the U.S. than anyone else had. He, in turn, blossomed in her care, as did the other neighborhood children who knew that Curtis's grandma was home every day after school serving cookies, milk, and fun.

By the time Dad and I returned from our commitments to the outside world, Mom handed me a healthy, happy child, always clear that, "now that your mom's home, she's in charge." Just as my grandfather living with us in Germany

had been an expanded safety net, never a substitute parent for me, Mom did not assume a role other than Omi for Curtis. We retained the boundaries of our primary relationships. Mom and Dad continued their intimate evenings, weekends, and vacations, while Curtis and I matured together. My parents were so intent on furthering our independence (and their own privacy) that they made a hefty down payment for us on a lovely three-bedroom ranch house a few blocks from theirs. For most of thirty years, Curtis would call that house home. I knew on that July morning in 1974, when we hauled our few possessions through the front door, that I'd be thoroughly content to live there until someone carried me out feet first.

IN FACT, OUR lives changed drastically within five years. Long before my father realized it, Mom had already suspected that our move to the Promised Land might not have been the panacea to lighten the personal and professional darkness Dad had tried to leave behind in Germany. She nevertheless gratefully acknowledged that our adopted country and culture had genuinely accepted us. With a few neighborhood acquaintances, Ute's growing family that had already provided Mom with a son-in-law and two grandchildren, and Chris and Curtis as almost constant companions, Mom found fulfillment in nurturing her relationships.

Dad's expectations, on the other hand, always needed more grandiose expression. Such ordinary accomplishments as a thriving household could not satisfy him in the long run. He despaired that in mid-life his valuable but unspectacular academic contributions had not brought him the research distinction he had expected. In a desperate effort to escape his imagined failures and start anew, he divorced his wife of almost forty years, married a bright, beautiful doctoral student more than thirty years his junior, and left his first family reeling from the blow of his rejection.

It wasn't just my father's physical absence that shook us but also the loss of his previous "larger-than-life" role in our world. With his thinly veiled insecurity feeding a ravenous need for approval, Dad never allowed even minor disagreement, let alone outright criticism, to be expressed in opposition to any of his views. Knowing him well, Mom had supported this fragile man's *sensitive* nature without question, trusting that he would always be there to protect her in return. I did the same willingly, because I never recognized Dad's certainty about everything for the hollow bravado it was. We instead would all silently agree that his sweeping assertions were what he claimed them to be: *the truth*. Though the price of pretense is high and we would all, including my dear Dad, pay dearly for our acquiescence, it was late in life to learn that lesson and recover, especially for Mom.

In fifteen years of effort to create a new life in the U.S., Mom had never worked outside our home. She had never learned how to drive a car. And for forty years, she had not made a personal friend, planned an outing, or considered a thought that wasn't shared first with her husband. In the vacuum created by his departure, the question was far from rhetorical: what *shall* we do with Mom? How can we stop her from literally disappearing into the void?

As I was, by then, attending the University of Colorado pursuing a Master's degree in religious studies and working, life was not exactly financially stable. Curtis wasn't yet ten years old. And although he shared his little family's anguish as he became a strong and compassionate young man, at the time he was still a child without either a father or a grandfather. He could certainly well use another adult besides his mother to help him grow up. Since my parents had succeeded in their goal to make me independent, only in my late twenties when Dad left, I was horrified at the notion of having Mom "move in" with Curtis and me. When friends suggested building an independent living unit onto our house, however, that alternative made as much sense as anything else we could think of. Looking back, it is clear that the addition of both Mom and her living space shaped our future—very much for the better.

Mom accepted a job in the cafeteria of a local high school to be home when Curtis returned from school. I could drive Mom where she needed, or we both wanted to be. From grocery trips to weekends in the mountains, the three of us planned family excursions that Mom, without a car, and Curtis and I, without the money, could never have taken separately. To my surprise and great relief, I discovered that Mom insisted on at least as much privacy as I thought I needed. Although the door

24

connecting our two living units generally stayed open to allow pets and Curtis to easily cruise between the two "houses," Mom and I unfailingly knocked before entering one another's space. We cleared shared times with the other's plans and only ate together during agreed-upon meals. The three of us quickly learned we had the best of both self-sufficiency and support; and while I'll never say that Dad's decision to leave us was a good thing, he did give me the tremendous gift of getting to know and appreciate my mother for the person she was beyond his shadow.

Two bus routes served our neighborhood in Boulder. Making friends with drivers and fellow riders, Mom grew more independent by becoming the expert on local public transportation. She could easily navigate the routes to her closer destinations, such as hairdresser, shopping centers, downtown Boulder, and church. She would just as easily take on longer trips to Denver, and the airport, or to visit friends who had moved from the area.

When an elderly friend had to leave her Boulder house for a nursing home many miles away, Mom tackled the five-hour round-trip bus journey with multiple connections and route changes to continue visiting her. Implying that anyone who would take on such a trek by public transportation was someone special indeed, Thekla would parade Mom through the dining hall of her new home and proclaim proudly, "This is my friend Ilse. She comes to visit me *by bus!*" For decades, Mom was known throughout our neighborhood and beyond as the German woman walking tall and steady to get any place she urged her feet to go.

Curtis attended all of his K-12 grades in our neighborhood schools. Despite being raised by two white women, he was nevertheless surrounded by a marginally diverse community thanks largely to the presence of a major research university. Folks in town recognized Curtis for who he was rather than for who people might assume him to be from his appearance.

We only made the "black boys love football" mistake once. During an early season scrimmage, I sat in the bleachers at the Baseline Junior High football field watching young kids, unrecognizable in their grotesque uniforms, being bullied and barked at by adults: "Get out there and get him!" Following orders, Curtis duly pounced and "got him." Rather than satisfaction, though, I saw tears welling up in his eyes as he ran over to me in the next time out. "Mom," he sobbed, "I hate it when I have to hit someone." Personally, I would have more likely said that I hate it when I get hit, but Curtis thought about the other guy first. We took his helmet off for the last time that very moment.

Curtis turned his attention to non-contact sports, playing soccer, running track, and lettering in cross-country. In junior high he created a painting his art teacher entered in the New York Gold Key competition. It won the honor, and the drawing still hangs framed in our study. In high school, he discovered volleyball. That sport is still his passion, largely because, as he once explained to me, "You have to figure out how to beat the other guys from your side of the net without ever touching them." He excels at combining finesse and strength.

For twenty years, Mom, Curtis and I got older together. They were good years, and while Curtis knew to expand his horizons out and away, Mom and I grew into the love and respect we would come to have for each other as women. But no, my mother had not always been my best friend, not even my favorite parent. Not by a long shot. It was just part of the most natural progression of our relationship that made me become my beloved mother's caregiver.

I've learned that I, too, am a link in this lineage of strong women. I am a privileged member of a family of matriarchs who knew, long before the concept and language of "unconditional love" became popular, that Home is where people are protected. It is where they are taken care of and in turn learn how to take care of each other. No matter what, it is where they are loved. The scars we still bear taught us all that the outside world will soon enough inflict life's painful, hard lessons. Home, by definition, is where you are safe. As Mom and I were taught by our mothers, that's how I raised my son from the beginning. And it's how I cared for my Mom to the end.

Sea Change: 2000

"We all have our White North"
–Ernest Shackleton

FOR USHERING IN the third millennium AD, the year 2000 was memorable in its own right. Prophets of all persuasions, from Christian apocalypticists to technological doomsayers, were issuing dire forecasts throughout the late 1990s. They warned that our lack of preparedness on all levels would seriously impede our gliding flawlessly into the twenty-first century. Predictions ranged from the drastic, citing evidence that the Rapture was imminent, to more general warnings that, at least the lesser gods ruling our lives would assert themselves by thoroughly disrupting our electronic and cybernetic connectivities.

Y2K became a universally understood watchword with, "Are you Y2K compliant?" code for modern civilization to "be prepared." It meant little more than, "Will you survive when the computers ordering our lives misinterpret those ominous three zeros in a row (2000) and refuse to send their appointed signals to the power company?" People's responses varied widely, but generally, their reactions were of two distinct types. There were the more fearful, who chose to cancel plans and stick close to home with water stored in bathtubs, cans of soup in the cellar, and propane stoves in their garage; and there were the outwardly defiant flaunting their "Who cares?" with particularly outrageous ideas for celebrating that New Year's Eve.

Since a millennium change occurs only once in very many

generations, few ignored it altogether. Even the quiet, "evening-at-home" crowd, generally not alarmist or excitable, still planned commemorative gatherings; and most everyone took at least minimal precautions to ward off the effects of a possibly colicky electronic transition from the second millennium AD to the third. We did so. With Mom still living more or less independently at the time, I had planned an early evening celebration together. But by midnight we had all settled into our own homes with a few preparations. Standard recommendations called for having a functioning flashlight, bottled water, and an extra warm nightgown—January nights without heat can get cold in Colorado!—close at hand. Just in case.

I said that Mom was living *more or less* independently. I have earlier mentioned my final name-change. After more than twenty years in the same house, fifteen of them living there with Mom, I did commit to another adult relationship. In 1995, I moved across town to live with my beloved Paul, in a sun-soaked, open house on a hill about as far north in Boulder as Mom was south. By the time I made that switch, Paul and I had known each other over a decade and loved one another from the start. Heaving a collective sigh of *finally*, fourteen of our nearest and dearest loved ones (including Mom, Curtis, and Ute) participated in our promises to making the transition into the new century together as a family last for the rest of our lives. Though married, I did keep Mom's and my ritual of ending my workday with a cup of decaf and a short visit before heading for my new home across town. It felt good just to check in with her and catch up.

Curtis was by then back in Boulder. After graduating from high school, he left Colorado for a small liberal arts college in Kansas on an art scholarship to receive his BA in elementary education four years later. His student teaching and certification were followed, however, by his perfecting another skill Curtis had developed while earning a small paycheck at college as a volleyball coach. He moved to southern California to train and partner with mostly blond, blue-eyed, trust-fund babies to gain admission to that lofty brotherhood of the American Volleyball Professionals. He spent years "on the road" making his living as a professional player in that international two-man sand-court sport he truly enjoyed. He was as success-ful as everyone expects an African American man to be in ath-

letics. He would jubilant-ly call me after another high placing in a nation-al competition. Yet more often than not our calls (usually made while he waited at an airport for a cheaper "standby" seat) would end with us wistful-ly laughing away the fact that his chosen path left him somewhat ill at ease. He was successful but dis-satisfied, and to explain his malaise we concluded most of our conversations repeating Lily Tomlin's pithy quip. "The trouble with the rat race is that, even if you win, you're still a rat."

Curtis had heard, of course, that all the players on the Tour tire of the rigorous traveling schedule required of profes-sional athletes. But since sports would never be Curtis's only love or talent, diverse interests as well as a healthy dose of *Niwot's Curse*[4], saw to it that home kept a strong hold on him. By the late 1990s, he was back to pursue a Master's degree in writing and poetics at Naropa University. But, how could he afford to go to school full-time and pay rent in this increasingly expensive town?

On some level, the answer was obvious. He needed an

---

4   The grip Boulder seems to have on those who apparently cannot leave once they see and experience it, or if they try, are doomed to return, is named for the great Arapaho Chief, Niwot, who lived in and loved this land long before the Europeans "discovered" it.

affordable place to stay. His dear Omi, having grown weary of renting to strangers the space I'd vacated, but still preferring someone nearby (especially at night), needed a housemate. Since Curtis could easily help out by driving, running errands, and providing a beloved male presence, Mom was delighted to have him back and gladly accepted a smaller rent income to have her grandson near. Curtis in turn enjoyed paying a reasonable monthly rent and some "in-kind" services as he moved back into his childhood home. It worked out well. Mom was living independently, while having someone upon whom she could depend close, but not so much so as to make either of them uncomfortable.

So, on December 31, 1999, the day of this momentous calendar shift, Mom had her things and family in order as always. She slept as the earth traveled uninterrupted through orbit, and computer clocks around the globe hit midnight to roll into the year 2000 with hardly a hiccup. Ignoring its inhabitants' fears with the same nonchalance as their dreams, the world simply went along. And if our family's transition into this brave new world may have been smaller in scale, it was no less memorable for us.

Late in 2000, I turned fifty. By another one of those lucky twists of fate (I call them blessings) punctuating my life, my people believe it appropriate to celebrate, rather than hide or deny, the marking of our time here on earth. I obliged by being born in November. One of the coldest, grayest months along North Sea shores, it routinely darkened days and spirits so that family and friends alike gratefully awaited my birthday every year as the occasion for a party—in my honor! Not an extravagant affair, the sweet smell of Bienenstich[5] from the kitchen and a vase filled with bright flowers on the table would greet me as I got up and affirmed that day when everyone genuinely commemorates your being alive. Every birthday was an occasion for the celebrant to feel important.

Your wishes directed the day, though I think my sister

---

5   Why my favorite, crusted-butter custard almond cake should be called bee sting has gotten lost somewhere in the generally logical German language tradition.

still hasn't quite forgiven me for how I, in her opinion, would squander my birthday privilege by choosing, of all things, tomato soup for the evening meal. In my defense, I maintain that those who have tasted my mother's tomato soup would understand! Birthdays honoring another decade of life, of course, brought even more than the *normal* fanfare. Once on to the game, dear Paul rose to my "Fiftieth" with a picturesque handmade brochure for a birthday trip to Costa Rica. We would fly south on January 1, 2001.

That special birthday in 2000 turned truly remarkable when, after far too many years (considering his fragile health) of intentional silence, a huge bouquet of flowers arrived from my father and his wife in Pennsylvania. The gesture, and my subsequent thank-you call, re-established muted, but at least formal, communication between us. When he suffered a massive stroke only three weeks later, Dad's birthday gesture had paved the way for a more genuine reconciliation before his death the following summer. With such gifts, I began the theologically prescribed, rather than merchant-dictated, *waiting* of Advent 2000 with even more joyous anticipation than I normally feel when I turn Christmas ideas into events.

It was this holiday season, though, that brought the first undeniable suggestion that all was not well with Mom. The change might have passed unnoticed if Mom hadn't been the consummate planner she normally was. Mom's need to order and manage her world might have begun in her late teens and early twenties as it was rapidly spinning out of control under Hitler's maniacal rule. But whenever its origin in her, planning ahead in our family was forever "Mom's way of doing things."

Although Dad, her kids, and eventually even grandkids offered Mom rides, she never drove a car herself and spent her life depending on public transportation. The penchant most of us have for squeezing just one more task out of the clock before leaving the house, hoping for a run of green lights or smooth traffic to regain lost minutes on the drive, was not in Mom's experience. That inclination has made me late or arriving breathless for more than one meeting. So I won't call the ability to drive our car, that all too often translates into an anxious rush too late

31

out the door, an unqualified privilege. However, always having to be exactly on time wasn't one for Mom either. If she missed the train or bus, they were gone. Traveling on their schedule, she would have to wait for the next one. So she learned to plan ahead and leave early so that I never knew her to be late for even the most trivial appointment.

Anything important, of course, would be scheduled, planned, and organized for months in advance. And it wasn't only out of Mom's firm conviction that everything in life just *goes better* if properly planned; it was the planning itself that brought her satisfaction. There weren't any spontaneous surprise *anythings* for Mom! A large part of the pleasure of any special occasion for her was living and reliving the anticipation that grew with careful attention to every detail.

Our marvelous family vacations were among the best of her gifts to us. For the summer, fall, and spring holidays we would spend in southern Germany, Switzerland, and Austria, Mom's planning landed us in many a special spot. That was no mean feat since accommodations in the continent's romantic, warm places filled up quickly. They were booked well in advance by sun-starved northern Europeans. Mom nevertheless could play (and win) with the best of them to score for us annual trips to the Schwarzwald and Allgäu, Jungholz and Zürich. All are names that to this day call up memories for me of wonder-filled, happy, and smoothly orchestrated family vacations. I still search for a chilled fruit soup as delicious as the one I would choose for dinner at the Berghotel Tirol after a long, well-planned  day's drive to our favorite destination in the little Gasthaus Zobel where we rented rooms above the barn. Warm and comfortable, we were lulled to sleep by the murmurings of satisfied, recently milked cows bedding down below our bedrooms.

Whether for trips across town to dental appointments, a

whole new country to explore, or an afternoon picnic, a mom who did not hold the schedule of what was happening when, *exactly* and clearly in her mind, was unrecognizable to me. And so it was until my fiftieth Christmas.

As I SAID, holidays were important in our family. In Germany, the magical day of the Christmas season is the twenty-fourth, not only for its religious significance, but because for us kids that was also when all the other good things happened. In our tradition, we would see the tree, lit up with real candles, and the gifts displayed only AFTER church and dinner on Christmas Eve. No electric lights and wrapped packages to wonder at for weeks ahead; on the evening of the twenty-fourth, when the scene was finally revealed, it was all as new as were the baby and the star millennia ago. And if American parents of children a certain age can forget about a good night's sleep before Christmas morning, German parents are similarly driven to distraction by kids willing the minutes to pass and turn Christmas Eve day into, well, Eve. For the whole family it was unbearably long.

Dad's gift to Mom was to get me out of the house that day. It was a gift to me too because in order to be out of Mom's way as long as possible, he and I would visit his office at the University in Hamburg. Driving there and back from our home in Aumühle would occupy at least two of the interminable daytime hours, and it was fun once there. As a linguist, Dad had a workspace filled with scientific specimens. For a little girl, even one who thought herself pretty familiar with remains and reminders of the natural world, walking into his lab reliably forced me to catch my breath, at least until my nostrils and lungs adjusted to the acrid smell of preservatives.

I took in the skulls and skeletons. I scanned the wall charts showing how the tongue, brain, and lips work, and wondered at rows of containers filled with biological samples—frogs, worms, and unidentified body parts forever incarcerated in their opaque caskets. But my eyes would search the shelves until they found what I really wanted to see again, just, I suppose, so I could say I had. I focused on the shelf with the jar containing a yellow, hardening human fetus floating in alcohol. If I never understood its significance in the science of speech development, I was spellbound by the suspended figure's curled position looking almost cozy, as if still in the womb. And I marveled at the tiny thumb, imperfectly formed but perfectly aimed, reaching toward the mouth in that apparently universal gesture of comfort and nourishment. Oh yes, the trip to the University lab was just exotic enough to distract me through that endless day and make me tolerable for my long-suffering parents. For me it was simply memorable.

By the time we returned from Hamburg, Mom's uninterrupted hours would have allowed her to prepare the house. Everything was impeccably planned, of course. The dinner table was set and the carp, which would be boiled and served with butter potatoes for the feast, was in the kitchen sink soaking in vinegar. I stared at each glistening scale, willing the silver to change colors, knowing full well we'd be no closer to dinner (followed by presents!) until the whole fish had turned an iridescent blue.

But it had time. Since Ute sang in the church choir, we next headed off to church. I loved the music and being with my family and just when the "church" part of the service got too boring, one of the candles on the tree in the sanctuary would start to ignite the branch above it. Billowing smoke and the pungent smell of burning pine needles caught the attention of the two ushers posted on either side of the tree. They would spring into action quickly to extinguish the little threat. Given the damp, cold climate of northern Germany, I can't imagine any tree could have ever gone up in flames. But even imagining the possibility sure made those services interesting. Anything to make time pass more quickly!

Finally, we would be back home. The fish would have completed its transformation, glistening blue in the sink. It wouldn't be long now. Still, say what you will about the daily rotation of the earth, a minute's perceived length depends on when in your life it is ticking by. Those last hours before we got to see the tree and our presents may have been only a fraction of the weeks of anticipation, but they were interminable! First we had to endure a festive dinner. Then Ute and I were banished from the living area, each to our own bedroom to wait. Thanks to Mom's careful preparations it was only moments, of course, but sitting alone I would force myself to read, or play, or do something other than wait for the seconds to drag by. And then that sound! Mom rang a small copper bell calling us in, hastily issuing a last set of instructions as we rushed toward the door: "Jani, your presents are on the large chair." "Ute, yours are on the couch." And all things warm and wonderful were revealed before my eyes. Trying to take it all in at once, I saw my bounty for the first time. The gifts were neatly laid out on the big chair right beside the tree glistening with candles, sweets, and decorations. The waiting was always worth it. Mom's planning saw to that!

Delicious if unbearable, we kept this routine alive through the years all three of Mom's grandchildren were little. It is a testament to its enduring value that one of the few things my nephew Michael claimed from his Oma's house when she died was the little Moroccan bell that used to summon the three of them, after church and dinner, into the living room, each guided to his or her appointed area of plenty.

Much later, with Colorado serving as a somewhat central location between my sister's home in Oregon, my niece and her husband living in Oklahoma, and Michael with his family just north of us in Fort Collins, I did all I could to assume the role of family matriarch. I never could re-create those family occasions exactly as they were imprinted on my memory. But I've come to enjoy the planning, shopping, preparing dinner, and the tree, now lit with electric lights and wrapped presents underneath for everyone at our house.

DECEMBER 24, 2000 was a Sunday, and eleven people gathered around our traditional dinner table. Glad of her help, I'd brought Mom to our house early, and we had already spread the preparations for chopping and measuring and baking all over the kitchen when the phone rang. Years of neglect had severely damaged the Christmas Eve day intimacy my Dad and I had shared until my teens. But in this fiftieth year since my birth we learned that our inattention to each other had not been able to completely destroy it. It was a pleasure therefore, to hear my Dad's voice continuing our halting efforts to show how much we really did remember those trips to his office. And how much they had meant to us.

But it had gotten late in life for words. My father's serious stroke a few weeks earlier had left him largely paralyzed and aphasic. I knew that and was prepared for it. Still, it tested my equanimity when we ended our conversation, his voice desperately familiar, now feeble and halting while searching for the right ending, until he finally uttered: "Happy Birthday, Chris."

I swallowed hard, barely beating back the gathering tears to stutter, "Merry Christmas to you too, dear Dad." We would have several more such phone conversations. I even saw and touched him during a healing visit just days before he died. But those words would remain a sharp reminder of all that is lost, and yet somehow retained, over a lifetime of living. A milestone at fifty.

Rejoining Mom in the kitchen to continue our Christmas Eve preparations, I took a deep breath to recover from Dad's call. Much needed doing, and we got to it. Mom was already dicing the apples that made her red cabbage the ever-requested complement to the Cornish game hens we'd chosen for the main meal. They would be festive, tasty, and not produce mounds of leftover turkey. Usually I love soups and stews served on the second day at least as much as the first time around. Maybe more. But this family feast would be a one-day affair. Christmas Day, the twenty-fifth, would find family members back home celebrating with other family and friends. As was our custom, Mom, Curtis, Paul, and I would eat at a favorite restaurant. No cooking, no dishes, and no leftovers for later.

This year all that post-holiday food was even less desirable. Just a week later, Monday, January 1, Paul and I would be off on my birthday trip to Costa Rica. So, for all the right reasons, including my three-year-old grandnephew's approval, "Um, I *like* these little chickens,"—game hens it was. The rest of the evening flew by in a whirl of gifts, music, and kids anxious to get home with the vain hope that the sooner they got to bed the sooner it would be their real Christmas morning. After a full day of people and activities, we dropped off to sleep much later and more exhausted than usual. But, with no little ones left in the house, we knew Christmas morning could start slowly.

One of the first things I did the next morning was to call Mom to wish her a Merry Christmas. "I'll be over soon to pick you up for the day. The eggnog and rumballs are ready and waiting." Mom sounded like a stranger as she tried to reconcile what I had just said with what she knew to be true: "What do you mean? I thought you were leaving today." Something inside me lurched as one's stomach aches during those rare moments when we recognize events to which all our future life experiences will refer. Mom didn't know it was Christmas morning? We had long planned to spend the day together. We *always* did. For a desperate moment, innocence was lost, and all the reasonable pretense that soon returned to grant me cover again evaporated with the realization that something was terribly, inexplicably wrong.

I don't mean to sound overly dramatic. All of us have gotten days and weeks confused. We've had the calendar turned to the wrong page and arrived on one date when our appointment was for another. But in some very basic, visceral way, I knew that that was not what was happening here. In all the weeks we'd been talking about the trip to Costa Rica, it was never suggested that Paul and I would be gone over Christmas—because we would be home, as always. And anyway, this was Mom, the queen of organized planning! She would never, not ever not know that this was Christmas morning, the Monday on which her family is going out for a holiday dinner; *next* Monday, she

37

would know, is when they are leaving on a trip.

Well, never before, that is. I pictured Mom sitting in her living room, calendar before her at the phone opened to Christmas week, just as it had been left there a day earlier. I'd sketched a green Christmas tree with red balls and a yellow star across the large calendar squares for the twenty-fourth and twenty-fifth, then written "Dinner at Paul's & Chris's" onto the first square, "Dinner at the Red Lion" on the second. It was clear as it could be to all, except Mom, who looked straight at it and could not sort out that this was, yes, a Monday. But Paul's and my departure for Costa Rica was scheduled, and also clearly marked, on a different Monday one week later.

Several years later, the neuropsychologist would explain the difference between the "normal" forgetting that happens to us all, and what goes on in the diseased brain: "We all forget where we put our keys, but it's something entirely different to have our keys in our hands and not know what they're for." I didn't know it then, but *that* was the difference I witnessed that Christmas morning for the first, horrifying time. My mind's eye pictured Mom staring at the open pages of her calendar, pictures, notations, and messages all clearly visible, yet unable to figure out what was happening on which day.

What I did know, or maybe sensed more than knew, was that we were headed for new experiences and that I had better get ready and prepare for I-didn't-know-what. Wherever I was going, I was pretty sure that the bright, tropical clothing I had begun to gather next to the backpacks for our Costa Rica trip a week later would not be appropriate attire for whatever awaited me on our arrival back home.

₳pproaching Ɖenial: 2001

*"Some people are always grumbling that roses have thorns.
I am thankful that thorns have roses."*
–Alphonse Karr

THEN THERE WAS the time early in 2001 when Mom reported getting on the wrong bus and ending up at that route's scheduled stop, rather than her intended destination. Twice. Occasionally we noticed that there was something about her gait, especially with her right foot shooting out in an awkward movement that was utterly unlike that lifelong proud and stable walk of hers. Mom's gaze on us sometimes felt more searching and lingering.

But while there were regular reminders, on the whole Mom's journey into memory loss was not a consistent downhill slide. The human mind's descent into dementia is an unpredictable trip with emotional tossing and tumbling. But for us, that jumbling of nerves was always interspersed with stretches of relative calm when one could pretend that things were normal. Each period of calm offered some respite before the next storm tested our resolve, and throughout, the conscious pursuit of familiar, happy routines allowed us some sense of normal life.

Mom was raised in the crowded tenement section of Hamburg's "Arbeiterteil," the clearly recognizable working-class section of that city of several million, the third largest seaport in the world. She was nevertheless destined to love Nature by inheriting her father's inclination toward the natural world, and through a benefit of his employment. Opa Vagt began

39

that work on the railroad in 1900, at age seventeen. By the time my mother was born in 1923, he had been a full-fledged member of the *Einheitsverband der Eisenbahner Deutschlands*[6] for five years. One advantage of union membership was a free rail pass for all family members. Thus Mom was not trapped, like so many of her friends and schoolmates, in the concrete canyons of inner-city Hamburg. Instead, she and her parents could spend almost every weekend in Dassendorf, a few houses huddled to call themselves a village, about an hour's train ride into the countryside around Hamburg.

With his own hands and limited material resources my grandfather had built a small cottage there, which they regularly visited. After the long train trip, they still had to go miles to reach their cabin. Sometimes they rode their bikes. Usually they walked. Either way, every

Dassendorf, Germany

visit entailed a long trek through the woods, often lugging the provisions for their stay. Mom loved every step and every minute there. She picked blueberries in Dassendorf, and mushrooms. She harvested the potatoes and asparagus her dad carefully planted, and she learned to cook and bake on the huge, temperamental cast-iron stove that dominated the small one-room structure. Her classmates, violin lessons, and, in her late teens, her only love, my dad, were all in Hamburg; but Dassendorf, with her parents awaiting her, is the home to which she longed to return as her illness progressed.

Opa Vagt's love for the outdoors was passed on through the generations. It was quite a stretch for me at first, but with my hand firmly reaching for his, I started serious walking early in life. Since I was spared the upheaval of the two wars my grandfather lived through, and was too young to grasp his loss when my grandmother died, I can only guess what these walks with his youngest granddaughter meant to this taciturn

6 German Railway Workers Union

man. But they influenced me beyond measure. I still believe that there's absolutely nothing life can throw at me that I can't heal just by remembering that tall figure with the enigmatic smile and his rough hand holding mine, protectively striding beside me. Long after my hand has left his, I still wander in Nature. The proximity of our Boulder house to the Mesa Trail, a spectacular path along the foothills west of town, allowed me to pursue that solace as a runner. I've spent hours on such trails—alone, accompanied by a succession of life-long human and canine buddies or happily on foot, skis, snowshoes, or bicycles with Paul beside me. My pursuit became more disciplined as I trained for my first marathon. For all the pleasure I take in explorers' tales, the real joy for me is not in reading about but actually living outdoor adventures.

For his part, Curtis earned his living with an outdoor sport for many years. Once he was surrounded again by Colorado's natural beauty, he became an avid fly fisherman. It seems he inherited not only his great-grandfather's respect for land and water but also his aversion to killing. So, although we've heard many great tales of man against fish, Curtis only does catch-and-release fishing with barbless hooks. It doesn't look like we'll ever have a meal from his angling efforts. Fishing, for him, obviously has everything to do with being in the wild and very little with catching a fish for the pan.

It is perfectly logical then, that for Mom and me, a drive into the mountains remained a reliable and long-shared pleasure that brought relief to whatever ailed us. We did so frequently, and more often as we noticed the first signs of Mom's rock-steady mind slipping away. We went there so often, I could have let go of the steering wheel and the car would have taken us to the parking lot at Sprague Lake in Rocky Mountain National Park on its own. The rugged trail, sufficiently maintained to allow visitors to walk all the way around the glacier pool, gives spectacular views in any direction. Our dose of fresh air was always followed by lunch in Estes Park.[7] We never took for granted the privilege of living within a lovely forty-five-minute drive of the Continental Divide others travel thousands of miles to visit. We well understood why they come. Mom's memories flowed easily as soon as we got in the car and headed west, which from our home is straight uphill.

How many times had we made that trip up the canyon? A hundred? More likely many times a hundred. Yet unfailingly, weather, mood, and season would make the experience new and exciting for us. In fact we always chuckled at friends who insisted they really had no need to repeat that outing. "Oh, yes," they proclaim earnestly, "we've already seen *that*," clearly implying there was no reason to go again. However, only some of our laughter was directed toward those whose reluctance to return we simply couldn't fathom. We laughed just as easily at our own insatiable, or just sufficiently simple, appetite for seeing the same stretch of road and scenery every weekend without ever tiring of it and commenting, genuinely, "Oh, look how *different* it all looks *today!*" We would even order the same meals. Indulgently smiling waiters would record our order well before we asked for the smoked salmon salad for me, the Reuben sandwich for Mom. We must be terribly boring, we giggled conspiratorially.

Like mother like daughter: we knew what we loved and we stuck with it! The desire to remind ourselves of our similarities was, of course, at the heart of our outings. We craved the opportunity to renew our bond of effortless familiarity, which reliably allowed Mom and me to always know, though not necessarily agree with, what the other meant. It was that comfort of being known and understood by the other our Saturday trips to our "Stammtisch" ringed by the Rocky Mountains affirmed. Regardless of the struggles Mom and I had shared, and there had been hard times to be sure, a window-seat overlooking a small lake surrounded by aspen, with resident ducks and busy muskrats, provided solace for us longer than any other beloved routine.

---

7   In 1864, William Byers, editor of the Rocky Mountain News, named the village now at the eastern entrance to Rocky Mountain National Park in honor of his hosts, the Estes family.

Like the food and venue, the conversation, too, usually had a certain sameness about it. After twenty years, Mom was still incredulous—she simply couldn't believe that Dad had chosen to leave her, along with all this beauty and the privilege to enjoy it here.

"Too bad," she would begin, her gaze upon the stunning scenery around us, "that all this wasn't good enough for him." A mixture of grief and anger would pour from her. But neither our relationship nor the setting would allow our hearts to sink there, especially since Dad's tendency toward *Weltschmerz* (expression of romantic pessimism about the evils of the world[8]) had been obvious to Mom from the first.

"Well, I knew he was complicated right from the beginning. There was that day on the train, after all...." As young lovers and music students in Lübeck, Dad once proposed a particularly grandiose, but apparently sincere, gesture of dramatic darkness. He suggested they should hold each other and jump off the speeding train. In death, he ventured, they would preserve their happiness of that moment forever. Mom, even as a young adult madly in love, was more grounded than her fiancée and couldn't quite see the romance of the act. For that matter she wasn't convinced of the death Dad envisioned and instead pictured their broken, bloody, and barely breathing bodies beside the tracks. She certainly did not see happiness there. So she held his hands firmly in her lap, she recalled, and convinced him she'd really rather stay happy *and* alive!

"Lucky for Ute and me," I'd chime in, and mean it.

But any negative thoughts Mom allowed herself about my father were followed shortly by far more pleasant and honest reflections. It was just as easy, after all, to embrace the dear, passionate attributes Dad had as a husband and father. I certainly experienced them. And Mom could reminisce twenty years after his departure about the puzzling and totally seductive power of his gentle, artistic temperament. So, regardless of the tangents our conversations took, by the time we'd finished our wine-spritzers and settled for coffee and occasionally dessert,

---

8   *The American Heritage Dictionary, Second College Edition,* Houghton Mifflin Company, Boston, 1985

we'd return to the sad acceptance of what it means to fully love a person who was not, in the end, ours to change or help.

Mom always insisted on paying for lunch and gas. She thanked me profusely for, as she would always say, "everything you do for me." I, just as often, objected. I was in my fifties and married. After a decade in a professional position at the University, I really could afford my own lunches! Besides, I wasn't just doing Mom a favor; I also enjoyed our times together immensely. For all one's maturity and other loves, there's no comfort like that of being "Known" with a capital K. Having been understood, forgiven, and accepted for who I am throughout my life by one precious person, my Mom, had been a rare benefit. Why wouldn't I take every opportunity to suggest a drive and a meal together to celebrate our relationship? I was just as eager as Mom was to capture that closeness we both suspected and feared was inexorably slipping away.

WE DID MANAGE, or perhaps dare, to forget what was changing in Mom on many a Saturday morning drive. But even while hoping that being together in the places we loved could make everything right, that illusion would be shattered soon enough. Lurking barely concealed under our efforts to hide it, reality would soon reassert itself in another episode of total Unknowing. We caught ourselves reminding one another more and more frequently that forgetting is a normal part of growing older. And at any age, there's no shame in answering honestly, "I don't know." But it brought no lasting comfort as Mom became increasingly afraid of appearing foolish when, slapping her forehead in frustration, what she came to call her "empty head" would fail her. The process was brutal and relentless.

While Mom was graceful in defeat, she was also fiercely stubborn, though not as much so as her father. He would steadfastly refuse to cede the street, while walking tall and proud toward the occasional car in Aumühle, muttering that he had, after all, been there first. Mom had long given up trying to convince him to use the sidewalks for his own safety; but once I was old enough to walk with him he agreed to set a safer example for his youngest granddaughter. Alone, his habit of moving silently headlong into the opposition, no matter its size or power, never changed. And fully her father's daughter, once claiming a position, Mom did not yield it easily either. She continued to let her feet take her to the bus for her "favorite walk" along Boulder's Creek Path and the political discussion group and lunch at the Senior Center. She walked to her hairdresser, the grocery store, and to church for weekly Bible Study before taking the bus back home. She always preferred her independence to asking others for a ride. On weekends she'd often meet friends for special outings.

One such meeting distressed Mom enough that she mentioned it to me repeatedly, raising that gut-wrenching red flag of alarm higher with each telling. One sunny April morning, Mom and her friend Doris had been at the Farmer's Market downtown. They had gotten there, of course, by bus—the one that runs up and down Broadway. That bus had taken Mom to and from work daily for years and connected her to everything interesting and important in her life: her beloved walking paths and group activities, the downtown stores and post office, and the lovely campus of the University that had brought us to Boulder so many years before. It had also, to a large extent, kept us here. Even Paul's and my home lay like all her destinations, close to that bus line. She had relied on that route for decades and knew it like the proverbial back of her hand.

Always, except on *that* day. She and Doris were again riding by the distinctive former fraternity house, which, for being the University building where I then worked, had also become a source of much pride for Mom. Not only had I assumed a professional position in an easily accessible part of Boulder, I was carrying on my father's connection with the University. Above all, she was greatly relieved that Chris, having followed a circuitous path to arrive at that point, was at last earning a reliable paycheck. I was receiving benefits and had achieved the stable livelihood that had been absent far too long for a single parent during my searching student years. The building then housing CU's President's Offices was unique enough in appearance to be widely known by its address, 914 Broadway. As *my* University of Colorado workplace, it represented for Mom just about everything that was right and good, and finally secure, about our life before my marriage. We knew all it meant to us indelibly.

Until the day Mom didn't recognize it—that one Saturday morning when suddenly all its significance was lost to her. Mom was chatting with her friend on the bus, riding right past "914," when her friend asked, "Isn't that where Chris works?" And poor Mom, looking straight at the Tudor-style building, could not think of what to say. Her "empty head" refused to yield an answer. The structure stood bold and unmistakable before her eyes, but Mom's brain could not produce a response for her friend.

SHORT-LIVED AS it was, that memory lapse nevertheless put a serious dent in what was left of our pretense. Horrified, Mom told and retold her story during our coffee time that afternoon, and many afternoons thereafter. How could that happen? The terror in her eyes searched mine for some explanation. How on earth could she not know where Chris worked?

A stoic northern European, Mom had gutted through the many physical and emotional changes of her aging without benefit of professional advice or medication. But even though Mom had not seen a physician for almost thirty years, the "914" incident proved unsettling enough to get her to agree that the time was right to make a visit to her Kaiser Permanente health facility. Maybe something could even be done to help?

We found a partner in Mom's physician, but not a miracle worker. The doctor confirmed what we had thought: that beyond somewhat elevated blood pressure, Mom's body was strong, capable, and "healthy." But what was going on in her head? During the physical exam, the doctor told Mom he'd give her three things to remember—a food, a color, and a car—continue with his examination, and after a while ask her to repeat those three things. I've become careful about claiming that I'll "never forget" something, but I'm willing to wager that the doctor's "pizza, red, and Volkswagen" (in that order) will stick in my mind for a very long time. Mom's physician then asked her to draw a watch face with the current time on it. Mom did so perfectly and we heard him explain with gentle reassurance that persons with advanced Alzheimer's disease generally can't complete this task. They tend to bunch all the numbers in one area, unable to create anything even vaguely resembling a watch face, let alone one showing a specific time. Mom had done well with that task!

Next he gave Mom a thorough opportunity to discuss how she was feeling. She talked fairly freely. In addition to mentioning the normal changes aging forces on all of us, Mom voiced distress at my Dad's terrible suffering at the time. Following the stroke, his condition had been complicated by cancer of the mouth and throat. In and out of hospitals for ineffective treatments and surgery, it seemed obvious to us that he was dying a painful death. Saddened by Dad's suffering and realizing that his dying would be the end of the man she had never stopped loving, clinical depression began to emerge as a likely diagnosis of Mom's illness. Especially since, after much prompting, Mom was even able to remember two of the three items from earlier in the exam. Maybe pizza, we thought, was lost to her for being most foreign to a mind still focused on preparing home-cooked German meals.

Depression seemed an eminently reasonable diagnosis. It often mimics or disguises conditions that reduce one's ability to perform certain tasks by depriving the person of sufficient energy and desire to remember or react. It may also suppress the ability to actually do so. No one doubted that Mom's memory was a minefield. Hurt and confused by her divorce for decades, she was now also deeply angry with herself for caring about Dad at all. Living his new life, Dad had given no indication that he cared what had been happening with her.

With these conflicting emotions circling endlessly, head-to-tail like circus ponies through Mom's days and nights, the physician thought that an antidepressant might help. Armed with a bottle of Prozac and instructions to follow the directions carefully to assure Mom would receive the medication consistently, we left his office with a concrete treatment and hope.

This class of drugs, we learned, acts slowly on the body's physiology, and only when taken very regularly. We were warned that it could take weeks, indeed months, before the medication had been sufficiently absorbed by the body to regulate its blood chemistry. No matter, we had time and didn't expect quick changes. We breathed deeply and gratefully as everything seemed infinitely easier now that the problem had a label. It would be years before I fully understood Sue Miller's assessment in her inspired article, "Watching Dad Disappear."[9] She mentions there that same immense relief at having an explanation for her dad's strange behavior upon hearing a diagnosis of Alzheimer's. Then with her next breath she says, "We didn't know enough to dread it as much as we should have." At the time, Mom and I didn't either. All we knew was that a possible solution for her symptoms had been identified. Empowered, we were convinced we could handle the problem!

We believed that before long, spring's increasing daylight that encourages all manner of life to burst forth would bring added *joie de vivre* to us as well. With eight to ten weeks of stable dosing with Prozac, Mom would have that all-important chemical boost on her side. Finally, she'd be able to gain some distance from the sadness of Dad's decline and reclaim her own spirit and energy. Come July, we'd be packed and ready for our annual, spirit-lifting sojourn to the East Coast.

---

9   People Magazine, excerpt from "The Story of My Father," 4/14/2003, pp. 93-94.

Sailing in Uncharted Waters: 2001

*"It is not because things are difficult that we do not dare,
it is because we do not dare that they are difficult."*
–Seneca

TEN DAYS AFTER we first became lovers, Paul loaded up
his Peugeot and drove east for the place on an isolated eastern
Maine peninsula become wildlife refuge he calls "Paradise,"
and home every summer. But he didn't leave without urging
me to come visit him there. It's a good thing I never wanted to
fight it. Because if Paul's wise and sensual nature hadn't been
enough to make me fall hopelessly in love, Petit Manan would
have finished the job. It may be the North Atlantic's western
rather than eastern edge, but there is no denying that Paul's
house overlooks the same
rugged waters of my childhood. The Atlantic is recognizable regardless of where
its gray, heaving waves lap
at land's end, and the first
time I laid eyes on Pigeon
Hill Bay to be greeted by the
salty air and muffled foghorn
bleating into the night, I
knew I had come home. I've
known it ever since.

Mom overlooking Pigeon Hill Bay, Maine

It is a testament to Paul's sensitive understanding of
Mom for herself and our relationship that he knew the same

49

would be true for her. By the early 1990s, he'd invited Mom to join us in that haven. And she did so every summer for the next ten years.

So it was on the morning after Ute's phone call from Pennsylvania announced Dad had finally been able to let go of this life peacefully that Mom and I handed our tickets to the airlines agent to receive gate and departure instructions for Portland, Maine. With equal measures of sadness for the suffering my parents had endured in the past year and relief at knowing that in very different ways each seemed to finally have gained some kind of peace, I was ready to relax on our vacation as never before. That summer marked Paul's and my second wedding anniversary. So in addition to our usual days of walking, talking, sailing, and porch-sitting, Mom, Paul and I looked forward to celebrating August 1 at our favorite small restaurant in a tiny village on the peninsula just across the bay. We had booked reservations and eaten lightly throughout the day anticipating the evening feast.

Rather than festive in mood, however, Mom was both tired and restless. She spent much time on the deck *resting up* and staring endlessly at the expanse of island-dotted water visible in every direction. If she was a bit more listless than usual, we weren't unduly alarmed. They may have been divorced for twenty years, but nothing could convince Mom's shattered heart not to grieve Dad's passing. We had also gotten used to the fact that although Mom's Prozac regime seemed to improve her spirits somewhat, her overall energy level had dropped significantly. This was a side effect, we had been told, which might lessen with time. Or it might not. But here, anyway, it was not too worrisome. The Maine coast is spectacular and ever-changing. Poets, artists, and even casual observers can easily wile away spellbound hours contemplating the wonder of it all. Besides, I remembered well from our weekends at the North Sea just how much a day in the fresh, salty ocean air would wear one out. It can exhaust you, even to the point of seeing things that either aren't there at all, or are certainly not what you imagine them to be. That's all just part of a quiet day in Paradise!

Having already announced several times that she was

going down to "her" room for a nap, Mom remained seated on the deck, focusing intently on something in the waves of Pigeon Hill Bay sparkling immediately below. At last she stood, stared, and finally voiced her concern: "There is a dog out there."

"Really?" Paul and I looked up. Seals call those rocky ledges home, as do loons, cormorants, and rafts of eider ducks. More than anything else, we saw lobster buoys bobbing on their lines, and hundreds of rocks glistening in the sun were transformed into a new creation with every tidal ebb and flow. There was much, real and imagined, in those living waters. But no dogs.

"Yes," Mom asserted, "I see the head. And the eyes are watching us... over by those rocks."

We strained to look again. Although the ocean's edge is less than a hundred feet from the deck railing, we grabbed the binoculars and scoured the scene for a dog in distress. "Hmmm, yes, we see where that rock does look like a dog's head," we agreed.

Mom remained adamant and was in no mood to be dissuaded. "No! It's still out there, looking at us."

When Mom started taking her antidepressant, the doctor encouraged me to keep a careful record of how Mom was feeling and I made a mental note to add to it: make an appointment with Mom's eye doctor when we return to Boulder. But mostly I searched my mind for a way to calm her. Perhaps a legal angle would help. "This is a wildlife refuge, so dogs aren't allowed here off leash."

"Yes, okay," Mom murmured. While she considered that information, it was clear that her conclusion was not in the least affected by it. "I see it looking at us." Pointing, "There. Right there."

"Hmmm (we tried again), but you know, if a dog did get into the water, it would surely have gotten back out by now." If for some inexplicable reason someone's pooch had, on a whim, decided to go for a swim, it'd be quickly reminded of the error of its ways. None would be foolish enough to stay in those cold waters for long. The Labrador Current temperatures can kill mariners who've come to grief within ten minutes of landing in

51

the drink, all within sight of the saving shore.

Mom interrupted our explanation with, "But they have nice warm fur."

"Which," we countered, "would only become soaked to weigh them down and drown them. No, really," we were trying to be comforting now, "no dog would be out there struggling all this time. It would swim to shore."

Mom nodded and agreed reluctantly, "Yes, that makes sense." But ultimately she was unable to follow our explanation through to its logical conclusion. There could not possibly be a dog out there swimming, his face turned toward us. Yet, logic be damned, Mom saw a dog. Her disturbing perception fixed in her mind, she headed to her bedroom knowing there was one out there.

She was only somewhat refreshed after her rest, and our spirits were slightly dampened with concern. We nevertheless headed off for our six o'clock dinner leaving the dog to its own devices. For all we knew, it was still swimming in the bay while the three of us leisurely shared a singularly delicious, five-course meal. Paul and I definitely remember it as a nice change from our normal fare of crock-pot, fresh bread, and salad suppers. But for Mom the evening was, if not ruined, surely marred by the memory of a poor creature stuck in the water. Like the dog unable to extricate itself from its fate by either swimming to shore or drowning, Mom's empathy was no less bound to the image of something from which no explanation could free her.

But honestly, the more we thought about it—that one rock with the sun shining on it from just the right angle—it really did resemble a dog's head and could easily have been mistaken for one!

WILLING TO ACCEPT any explanation for what Mom saw that day, we didn't totally make peace with the dog episode either. Not too long after our return to Boulder, I revisited my scribbled notes from Maine and was able to talk Mom into having her eyes checked. The ophthalmologist assured us of what we knew: Mom's eyes were better than mine have ever been. She rarely needed her glasses and still had 20/20 vision; it was not Mom's eyes that had deceived her. But there was no dog in Pigeon Hill Bay that day.

Far removed from the heavy sea air, Mom remained tired to the point of incapacitation. And, whether from fear, embarrassment, or physical exhaustion, she was beginning to retreat from the active life she had led. Mom made no effort to resume her fall routine of planning favorite activities and somewhere deep inside, the relief I had felt with Mom's diagnosis of depression was fading. After five months of Prozac, she had not significantly improved and was actually showing some additional, disturbing symptoms.

That was especially worrisome since living together during our three weeks in Maine had allowed particular diligence in seeing to it that Mom got her medication in a timely fashion. We had been warned that any medication prescribed for the elderly, especially drugs as potentially volatile as antidepressants, must be administered under supervision to assure they are taken appropriately. Those containers with day and time compartments are handy. They *should* work. But even they required that Mom remembered to actually reach in there and take the pill thirty seconds after a reminder phone call. And they didn't help one whit when, while looking at the pill in the "Sunday a.m." compartment before leaving for church at ten, Mom vigorously insisted that, "I know *that* one is still in there, but I'm very sure I took my pills this morning. That must be from a different day." Could she have taken her medicine out of the prescription bottle? The one we'd hidden in her nightgown drawer?

Nothing was certain. Except that Mom was not at all well. By now we'd all accepted that our lives were being undeniably changed by her condition with the "effects of normal aging" excuse now failing to convince even Mom and me—the most desperate proponents of that explanation. They rang hollow for contradicting our observations and proved increasingly disrespectful of the degree of trouble Mom was having. The frequent instances of Mom's "empty head" remained disconcerting. She no longer needed to report them to us, as we were becoming regular witnesses to her inability to react or function properly.

At least we had been given a medical diagnosis and a treatment plan. When someone hands you a hammer, there's a temptation to treat everything as a nail. But we had accepted the depression diagnosis to mute our rising concerns because it was one that made sense with Mom's world. As her peers died, went to assisted living facilities, or moved closer to family, Mom's circle of friends was shrinking noticeably. Less physically able, she became steadily less interested in pushing herself to participate in life; for her, there wasn't much left to enjoy. Maybe Mom wasn't improving simply because, let's face it, her life wasn't either! Despite our best efforts to include her in a life worth living, with Dad's death just a few months past Mom began losing her internal fight for survival.

Though she tried to be as gracious about that loss as she had been about most else, Dad's death carried a breathtaking finality for Mom. Her struggle to handle Dad's death turned out to be infinitely harder for Mom than we had anticipated. We reasoned that Dad's desire for a divorce, his remarriage, and total absence from our lives had occurred twenty years ago, after all. But looking back more honestly now, any assumption of Mom's healing was our failure to understand the depth of her grieving. We knew Dad was, and had always been, Mom's first and only love. His demand for loyalty and attention had been uncompromising, and she had willingly given it. It would be more than twenty years into their marriage before they allowed some family or professional reason to force them to spend a night apart. I remember as a teenager, when Dad finally agreed to a lecture tour that Mom couldn't join, she willingly shared Dad's daily letters to her—but only to a point. We were not allowed to read them until she had prepared them by covering the intimate parts addressed only to her with masking tape.

Given our understanding of their life together before

the divorce, we should have realized that she had never relinquished hope of something personal from him. Did she long for an expression of regret? An apology? We didn't know, but it was very clear that, until she learned of his death, Mom didn't fully believe that he would really never return to her. His passing forced her to finally accept that no kind word of reconciliation, or hint of recognition on his part of what was lost when he left her, would ever come.

On the other hand, Mom was a bright woman. She had had no contact from Dad for twenty years. It would not be his death, she knew full and well, which would now keep him from communicating with her. Still, with new losses magnifying old ones, Mom spent that year following his death with little relief from her anger, pain, and consuming grief. And if we hated to see her so unhappy, we certainly understood and in some way shared her state of mind. In fact, I still believed that if she *didn't* feel saddened and overwhelmed at this point in her life, there really *would* be something wrong with her! Honestly. To my searching mind, the depression diagnosis served as encouraging proof that nothing was seriously wrong with Mom. She was, in fact, reacting quite appropriately to the increased loneliness and isolation of her world, wasn't she? Maybe Prozac just wasn't the right drug.

Looking back, hindsight and all, I should have known better. But most major life changes sneak up on us, don't they? Like a child's growth unnoticed until visiting relatives marvel at "how tall you've gotten." Or that morning when, seemingly overnight, the skirt that always slid so smoothly over your hips will now hardly close. Somehow the process of change insinuates itself into our awareness so slowly that it takes an unusual event or new observer to bring it to our attention. At this point in Mom's disease and diagnosis, we were neither physically distant nor emotionally removed enough to be those observers.

.

New Landscapes: 2001-2002

*"Do not save your loving speeches for your friends till they
are dead. Do not write them on their tombstones.
Speak them rather now instead."*
–Anna Cummins

IF WE WEREN'T questioning the depression diagnosis yet,
Mom's overall demeanor did convince us to seek a different
medication. Maybe something else would be more effective? The
doctor thought it worth trying another class of drug to which the
elderly respond well. Given that Mom's lethargy from Prozac
seemed to be adding to her confusion, we could hardly make
things worse by switching her to something called Wellbutrin. It
might even be the right thing. Wellbutrin accumulates quickly
in the bloodstream making its effects noticeable almost immediately. That sounded good, since we were banking on improve-
ments for Mom. We desperately needed evidence that something
would turn this thing around; and we needed it soon!

Not surprisingly, the medication change would have disad-
vantages. If we didn't want Mom on an even wilder ride of fluctuating energy than the one she was already enduring, she had
to get Wellbutrin precisely as prescribed. Without fail, we were
cautioned, the dosage must be administered morning and night.
And since even the "fail-safe" compartmentalized med dispens-
ers had in fact failed with Mom, Curtis jumped in to help by
taking the morning shift of the daily monitoring. It was already
his practice to go to his Omi's place to say good morning before
leaving for school every day, so it was easy for him to remind
Mom *and* watch her as she took her first dose of the day.

For my part, I had hardly noticed that my afternoon

visits, formerly social time shared between equals, had now assumed the suspicious regularity of intentional home visits. I was no longer comfortable going anywhere with Paul even for a day if it meant not seeing Mom in the afternoon. Our days of hiking and snowshoeing, and beloved hut-to-hut backcountry skiing and bicycle weekends fell by the wayside as I replaced not one but two teakettles for Mom in rapid succession. Each had been charred and ruined when Mom forgot to turn the stovetop burner off until well after all water had evaporated. Kettles with plastic whistle caps were not the answer either, since those melted when the kettle was left over the heat for even just a bit too long. As she would be embarrassed to let me know that she had forgotten the hot water for our coffee routine yet again, Mom would remove the whistles to leave the whole pot (or house) to burn the next time the red-hot burner was left on. A little slow on the uptake, or maybe just unable to give the final nod to reality, I didn't buy an electric kettle with automatic shut-off until the third replacement.

Paul bolted strategically placed handles next to Mom's entryway, as she was becoming less and less stable navigating the doorsteps. We installed a brace on her bathtub and removed all of her throw rugs. And since a shopping center was nearby, it was no additional hardship for Curtis and me to assume grocery duties. We did this not so much because Mom could no longer get to the store, but because more and more frequently she would come home clutching her list and some snacks, but not the needed items. We attempted to see to it that Mom continued her "normal" routine as much as possible, but providing nourishment, human interaction, and her medications regularly was requiring nearly constant attention. Even though we knew we could no longer assure ourselves of her safety, that didn't keep us from trying. With Curtis's, Paul's and my combined efforts, we brought out the cavalry to hold off the beast already nipping at Mom's heels and our hearts.

The fact that months of antidepressants had not worked so far did not reduce my determination to make Wellbutrin and our new routine work. Instead of allowing winter's darkness then settling on the land to also invade our souls, I enlivened my early evening visits with Mom with talk of *next* year. I had one more solution up my sleeve. We'd only been back several months from that difficult trip to the Maine coast, but mentally I was already planning for summer 2002. I was desperate, to be sure. But I am also my mother's daughter. Everyone who knew us both, including casual observers, recognized that immediately. But that was never more obvious than when it came to planning!

I was onto something. Current bereavement wisdom teaches that one of the most important aspects of healing life's wounds is closure. Sounds good in theory, but Dad's sudden departure, demand for a divorce, and subsequent total estrangement had never allowed his contact with Mom of any kind. Closure had been impossible for her to attempt, let alone achieve. Crippled by his own guilt, Dad had made no effort to excuse or explain his actions. Beyond blaming us for his aging and misery, he allowed no opportunity for communication as he sought escape from his own sense of failure. He simply fled and left us surrounded by the rubble of what used to be our emotional and physical home.

It's true there was nothing helpful Dad could have said at the time. He might as well have stayed silent, I seethed furiously to myself. Mere words, even his, could never have eased Mom's raw heartache as she watched him disappear to introduce his young wife to the Germany and beloved roots Mom had forced herself to abandon to support his hopes and dreams in America years earlier. She could only have felt utterly betrayed.

Still, the instructions in the divorce counseling manuals were clear: talk, mediate, confront, and grieve. Maintain your integrity by insisting on your rights and reasons, and never permit another to destroy your sense of worth. Regardless of how they treat you, your dignity is yours to keep. Fine advice, but helping Mom act on those ideals was beyond me. It is like understanding the concepts of light years and galaxies, for example. Something beyond mere knowledge is required for grasping them. I cannot comprehend such impossibly great distances. Likewise, for twenty years I understood well the logic behind the prescription for Mom's healing, but I felt powerless to help. Never mind that the guidebook was in my hand; I couldn't, as they say, "get there from here." The problem was, of course, never mine to fix.

BUT NEXT SUMMER'S trip, now *there* was something I could do! With maps and calendars in hand, I approached Mom enthusiastically to start looking beyond the cold, short days of January.

Hans-Heinrich Wängler, ca. 1995

"What about a flight to, say, Cleveland, next summer?" I began. Inspired, perhaps by Thelma and Louise's romanticized breaking free, I next suggested we could rent a car and take a road trip. Together we could handle the drive through northwestern Pennsylvania where Dad had last lived and so recently died. We'd visit his grave in the small rural cemetery that became his final resting place; after a short meditation or prayer, with his grave confirming that whatever had happened between Mom and Dad, his demons were finally calmed, we'd push on to Maine. There we could recapture our own peace. I clung fiercely to what had thus far saved Mom throughout her life. A plan!

As plans go, it was a good one that started smoothly enough. Our flight left Colorado on July 17, a year to the day after Dad's death. Following a drive of several hours through Ohio and northwestern Pennsylvania, we approached the area where Dad last lived and easily recognized the tiny cemetery beside the country road. As my sister had described it, right at the edge of the woods, we found his grave just as easily. Surrounded by lush vegetation, Dad would have loved the spot. While too green and closed in, threatening to suffocate the two of us who had reluctantly but fully come to thrive in the wide-open spaces of the West, Mom and I nevertheless agreed that the setting was lovely. Next we stared at the huge, black letters on the gravestone proclaiming broadly: Hans-Heinrich B. Wängler. The large formal script struck us as gaudy and thoroughly incongruent with the natural surroundings. Dumbstruck, I thought sadly to myself that he apparently still couldn't trust that his presence on this earth had left a lasting, loving impression without this monumental reminder. Mom uttered something about the striking absence of anything personal, as we searched the inscription, re-reading those vaguely familiar letters that yielded no hint of the deep passions that dictated so uncompromisingly all my dad ever felt or did. The loneliness of the gravesite was palpable. Even (or is that especially?) with his widow's name already inscribed for her to join him there upon her death, we found no evidence of the humanness of this remarkable, broken man. We felt a pity neither of us could express as we left one red rose to remind him, and ourselves, of the love that gave birth to my life.

The visit helped me feel better. It did little, I suspect, for my dad. And I wondered what Mom was thinking. Knowing that, though momentarily together, the three of us had each participated in this moment separately, Mom and I nevertheless turned away from the grave together. It was time to go. We walked back up the hill to the car—and our life—agreeing that this surely was the most peaceful place this deeply loved, conflicted man had inhabited in a very long time. Whatever we believed about after-death existence, this was a fine place for our final memories of Dad.

In the early evening light we waited at the cemetery entrance for an Amish family to pass, dignified in their simplicity, as they moved slowly along the road before the setting sun in their horse-drawn buggy. Leaving my father in this peaceful place, finally free of his raging demons, brought a lasting calm to me and my feelings about our complicated, passionate, and, in the end, doomed relationship. But love and atonement can bring comfort only as long as they are remembered. Although I didn't know it then, our visit could no longer offer anything of the sort to Mom's fading memory.

IT WAS ONLY a short drive to our lodging for the night where we arrived weary beyond words. Or maybe we just didn't know what to say. Mom went into the bathroom to "freshen up" while I explored possibilities for a quick dinner. I was on the phone with the front desk when I heard a dull thud, then a groan, from the bathroom. I raced over to see what had happened but couldn't get in. Mom, in her uncompromising need for privacy, never left a bathroom door unlocked. Damn!

"Mom," I said urgently, "are you okay?"

"I can't get up."

It took all I had to stem the rising tide of panic. "What happened? Where are you?"

"Don't know. I'm too tired to get up."

Sitting on the floor, I leaned against my side of the locked door. "Can you get your knees underneath you? Have you got something to hold on to? If you can just reach up to unlock the door, I'll come in to help you."

"No!" Now the panic is hers. "I don't have my panties pulled up."

Envisioning Mom robbed of her last scrap of dignity, I swallowed my frustration. From inside the door I heard, "Maybe I can do it."

There was hope, so I started to coach, "OK, Mom, really slowly..." when the click of the latch releasing freed us both. I carefully opened the door to find Mom slumped next to the commode, but now fully clothed. I remembered to breathe. Trying to help her get her feet underneath her while she struggled to get up, I realized horribly that it wasn't physical weakness that kept Mom on the floor. She had slid off the toilet and folded there where her brain couldn't unscramble the task messages that told her legs how to get up. Once I gently moved her legs into position, touched the appropriate muscles, and identified for her what to move and when, she was able to rise. Bruised, far more deeply than the purple welts already forming around her knees suggested, Mom sank into bed. With her settled and calmed, I fetched us some take-out barbecue. It tasted like cardboard.

Our three weeks in Maine brought much that was familiar to Mom. Aside from occasionally seeming ill at ease and insecure, she coped well. We, her friends and family, kept up the pretense of normality by encouraging her to rest, offering explanations, and pointing out familiar landmarks that helped orient her somewhat in a place that, even then, must have been more new and strange to her than we realized.

The time flew by until the sad morning we headed home to Colorado. Maybe I'm just immature. Or perhaps too many separations from family and friends have turned out to be permanent. Whatever the reason, I'm not good at good-byes. I get conflicted and despise ending our annual "fix" of the wooded, watery Maine world, even as I begin to long for the dry, high plains and mountains of home. It also didn't help that, while we never said as much, we knew that Mom would never return to Petit Manan Point. Her traveling days were over, and with that our thirty-year tradition of weekend trips and vacations together was coming to an end. Dreading that loss at least as much as the two-day drive back to Cleveland, I found this departure darker and sadder than our usual somewhat feigned, cheery, "We'll do it again next year!" We still said it, but no one meant it; and after blueberry pancakes and hugs from Paul, we finally headed the car up the driveway for Mom's last farewell. The sun sparkled on Pigeon Hill Bay. The Petit Manan lighthouse stood tall and silent on this bright, fogless day against the blue Atlantic; the road lined with lupine and neatly stacked lobster traps made this the quintessential Down East Maine of travel guides and magazine covers.

And that's just along the eight miles of winding, hilly road from the Wehr mailbox to Scenic Route 1. There, Mainers and "From-Awayers" alike must drive either northeast or southwest toward the coastal communities that had settled in Mom's heart. Northeast lies Lubec, the eastern-most point in the U.S. and a namesake, if not the same Lübeck where Mom and her newfound love, my dad, attended music school in Germany. Acadia National Park, Camden, and other picturesque harbor destinations are to the south. From Petit Manan there is no other way but U.S. Route 1 to get to those places. And we know how to reach them not by road signs and highway markers, but because familiarity guides us there. Farley Mowat claims to have first discovered this ability in Newfoundland fishermen. True natives of that island guide their boats safely to where they're headed without chart, radar, or other navigational aids. They can do so also without benefit of sight as landmarks are too often shrouded from view by fog. So how, in heaven's own name, Mowat mused, can anyone possibly find his way through the watery miles of impenetrable gray soup that constantly envelops these island people? As perplexed by Mowat's confusion as he was by their skill at navigation, one native fisherman's response is as simple to him as it is incomprehensible to "landlubbers." "Well me son, we knows where it's at."[10]

Along that drive down Route 1, Mom and I, too, had always known where we were. We could not, in fact, have mistaken it for anywhere else. At least not as long as we could remember the typical Maine scene every postcard immortalizes. Despite the fact that Mom and I had enjoyed that trek along the Maine coast together many times, her repeated questions that day, wondering fearfully where we were and awestruck by how I knew the way to Portland, opened my eyes to how much Mom's mind was leaving us.

We drove to Springfield, Massachusetts and arrived at our motel with Mom having absolutely no idea where we were, where we'd been, why we went there, or where we were going. Nothing. She couldn't recall that we had left Maine only a few hours earlier, and asked incessantly why we were sleeping at a motel rather than in our beds in Boulder, "where we were this morning!" Boulder? This morning? How could she have for-

---

10 Mowat, Farley, *The Boat Who Wouldn't Float,* Bantam Books, 1969, p. 60.

gotten that we left Maine several hours ago and instead think she had woken up in Colorado? *When*, I catch myself wondering fleetingly, did I become the adult in the car who knows where we're going as the children wail, "Are we there yet?" Whenever the change had happened, I wish someone would have let me know!

Once I heard the slow, steady breathing of Mom asleep in the bed next to me, I resigned myself to a tearful rush of self-pity. I turned the light on and distracted myself (or perhaps assured myself that I'd not lost my mind) by writing in my journal: "Trying to explain again and again where we are, what we're doing, and laboring to somehow bring some recognition to that empty landscape that seems to be Mom's mind, I'm exhausted, sad, and feeling utterly alone." Next, I picked up the phone and called Paul back in Maine. His voice and words soothed me across the miles and I found the courage to turn the light out again.

Our second day's drive on to Ohio wasn't quite as distressing. Neither of us had been to that part of the country. I treated Mom's reading and repeating every road sign and mileage marker we passed as orientation for us both, not irritated by her frightened effort to grasp some familiarity in a landscape she didn't recognize. A good night's sleep in an Erie, Pennsylvania hotel worked magic for us. We confessed that those Interstate highways could make anyone feel lost and confused, and we started our morning enjoying a truly beautiful walk by Lake Erie. We held hands as we reminisced. Reassured of each other's presence, we survived both the "car-rental-return-airport-shuffle" nightmare and the flight. Crowded and hurried, it was a far cry from the treat air travel used to be, but it got us to Denver. Bone weary we wandered, again hand in hand, through Denver International Airport until we saw Curtis's smiling face at the luggage carousel. We were assured by far more than his ability to handle our bags that we really would make it home! His presence brought the comfort a life preserver—heck no, a whole boat—must give to a drowning man. For the moment we were safe.

❦

WE LOVED OUR summer weeks in Maine for the pleasure it gave to be, well, in Maine. But an added bonus of our vacation there was that by the time we returned west, the scorching weather of July was waning. The midday heat was bearable because the sun was dropping behind the mountains a little earlier each day. The sleeveless tee shirt would no longer do as an early morning nightdress; it was time to snuggle into a bathrobe again for that first cup of coffee on the back deck. And the evenings were chilled once more by that crispness in the air that marks the nights here in our semi-arid, high-altitude region and makes living in this climate so pleasurable.

Like all of the life around us emerging from midsummer refuges in cool places to rejoin the world outside, Mom and I also resumed our cherished routine of coffee and treats in the shade on her patio. The neighbors' dogs once again had the energy to bark a welcome at my arrival. Robins, finches, and squirrels eagerly sought out the birdbath just a few feet from our chairs; and children's voices rang out from swings and sandboxes. Life, with a capital L, seeped back into the limbs of all as the setting of the sun brought relief.

Energy for work returned as well. From our patio, we had witnessed for years a girl's steady improvement as she practiced her violin with back door open just two houses away from us. We'd shuddered and cheered through endless repetitions of exercises and difficult sections of a particular score. I would watch Mom's hands, which still knew exactly where the fingers needed to be to hit that note precisely, moving in sympathetic labor, vicariously urging the student's hands into position. Then a small smile would light up her face. Whether the result was right on note, or, as all too often, slid in slightly sharp, Mom had always known the same potential for defeat or victory inherent in every effort.

With precious memories as fuel for our conversations, the patio lent a delightful intimacy to our afternoon coffees—until one late summer day when memories could no longer inform

Mom's reaction. Our young violinist was working through a particularly difficult but beautifully executed score, when in a burst of gut-level repulsion Mom suddenly exclaimed: "The violin really is a *terrible* instrument!" Maybe because I'd so often felt precisely that way, but never allowed myself to tell her so, I laughed out loud. Somehow the incongruence of this, to me, quite accurate observation, and Mom's lifetime of blind devotion to this instrument, made me laugh. But it wasn't a joke. Mom's eyes registered confusion at my outburst. I had misunderstood. At that moment, with only *that* moment to refer to, Mom truly did find the violin a "terrible instrument." She couldn't see what struck me as funny. Her expression remained lost and blank as I stuttered some excuse; "Well, I don't know about terrible. But it *is* awfully unforgiving, isn't it."

But to no avail. Far removed from the experience of the professional violinist and musician Mom had been for well over seven decades, she was now reacting to what she'd heard in the same immediate, visceral way I was. Right, there's been many a convoluted piece of music that's made me want to scream what a terrible instrument the violin is—but never before to my Mom!

Trying to understand Mom's completely uncharacteristic but genuine comment, I almost asked her something about maybe not feeling quite like *herself* that day. But I stopped short when I remembered a scene in the movie, *The Madness of King George*. The Prime Minister goes to visit the King, urgently wishing him to be better so that he might retake command of his country. Spotting his sovereign walking happily in the hospital garden, he greets him with visible relief: "You seem more yourself."

To which the King responds dryly: "I have always been myself. But I'm remembering how to *seem*."

The woman who sat by my side honestly disparaging an instrument she had once been able to make sing was clearly forgetting how to *seem*! I smiled at my beloved Mom in silence trying to recognize her for who she was at that moment. It was a lovely autumn afternoon in Colorado, but I felt a shiver run down my spine. I feared a cold, totally unfamiliar landscape awaited us just around the corner.

A Wrong Turn: 2002

"If you're going through hell, keep going."
–Winston Churchill

NOT ABLE TO shake the memory of that afternoon, I was afraid of the shorter days that mark the arrival of fall for the first time in my life. And that's saying something! For as long as I can remember, I have happily anticipated the arrival of autumn even more than I've looked forward to every new season. In firm opposition to friends who insist how much I would *love* living in, for example, Hawaii, I know that I could only really thrive in a location with four distinct seasons.

I'll confess to looking forward to even the bleak November skies of my childhood. The dark evenings meant it was time for *Laternengehen* parties. Noisy groups of children would light up the neighborhood by carrying burning candles inside beautifully crafted, brightly colored paper-lanterns on wooden sticks. Since Mom was always willing to serve as adult supervisor for these events, I benefited from participating in many such memorable evenings. Though it had a very different seasonal effect, our move to Colorado only served to solidify a youthful preference into an adult's firmly held conviction. Already well-established as a favorite time of year for me, autumn quickly became the high point once our roots were solidly planted in those foothills between plains and peaks.

Granted, winters are spectacularly beautiful in Colorado! Unhindered by clouds, the faithful sun brilliantly reflected on dry, high-altitude snow draws skiers by the hundreds of thousands to where our clear blue skies meet white, powdery slopes. But the cold, short days that turn too quickly into colder, long nights require gear and planning for all eventualities and make travel, whether merely across town or on our mountain outings, decidedly more difficult. Then there's spring, everyone's favorite season. Who doesn't hunger for more daylight urging buds and blossoms to "spring" to life? But while in many places spring is a slow, steady progression of increasing light and warmth, at an elevation of almost 6,000 feet in our eminently habitable foothills, spring is a colicky child. A willful creature, she takes those eagerly awaiting her arrival for a fitful dance. Seductively warm March days give way quickly to late-winter storms ruthlessly breaking the flowers, fruits, and branches, and occasionally the spirits, of those misled by a bit of warm weather to believe that it was safe to come back out and play. And then there's summer. Long days brimming with energy bring life and courage to all. But in July, that endless western prairie just to the east of us can get hot. And it can stay brutally so, until the skies finally release their accumulated energy in violent thunderstorms of lightning, rain, and hail. Or, just as often, they threaten death and damnation but produce no water at all for the thirsty land.

And so the year goes until early September announces the arrival of fall when the breezes wafting down from the Continental Divide take on a sharp edge that refreshes, rather than caresses, the face. There comes one last collective outburst of warm weather watching. "Please," goes the heartfelt plea of Coloradans, "no snow in the high country for our Labor Day picnic, family reunion, or camping trip." Everyone hopes to get out once more for that official Farewell-to-Summer ritual. Not I. For me the jewel of the year arrives with that first late-August evening when I need to put on my fleece snuggle-suit to enjoy our last glass of wine on the deck. That's when I wrap my arms around my knees, hunker down, and wait for dusk to bring the embrace of the season I love!

No more lugging extra clothing in our packs for suddenly plummeting temperatures and biting wind-chill on even the shortest ski trip. Behind us are the slogs with reluctant skis through the wet, melting snow of March. And best of all, banished to history are the power-charged lightning storms splitting the summer skies. Deadly in their unpredictability, they no longer threaten the earth, turning a summer hike above timberline into something like traversing a minefield. Putting an end to all that, late August ushers in several months of what is to my mind, Colorado's loveliest season.

Residents and visitors alike are justly moved by the profusion of color of New England's fall foliage. But on the *perfect* September weekend, Colorado also has its spectacular colors. People flock to the famed Peak-to-Peak Highway for a glimpse of the brilliant splotches of gold, peach, and wine-hued aspen leaves that blanket our hillsides. Do they marvel, too, I often wonder as people hop out of their cars for a quick photo-op, at just how fleeting the trees' moment of splendor—and ours—is in this life? I haven't gone through a fall without hoping that I might have a bit of the grace and beauty in my dying that the leaves show in theirs, as they glide slowly, inexorably, toward the ground to become the mulch for their re-birth.

That year, though, everything was different. Suddenly I didn't feel so philosophical about bright colors at life's end. Decline and decay were just too real to allow me to be so romantic. Rather than the customary festival of Nature's bounty before winter's hibernation, the ever-shortening days of autumn 2002 brought an impenetrable darkness. We must have taken a wrong turn. We were no longer traveling through the brilliant foliage Mom and I used to celebrate with annual viewing trips, but instead we found ourselves dreading the long shadows obscuring the fading light. And somewhere in the darkness, *"people"* had moved into Mom's backyard.

The telephone is too often a tiresome, unwelcome device in my life. In fact, I remember my years without it well. Especially the day my grandmother's brother, who had spent little time away from his rustic patch of land outside Hamburg, came to visit us in Aumühle in the late 1950s. We proudly showed him around our recently acquired home and he was pleased for us. His awe at our refrigerator and modern plumbing astonished me. But I was most impressed by his reaction to the bathtub's hand-held shower and hose above the faucet. Obviously unfamiliar with any "modern" indoor facilities, he took the shower

71

off its cradle, held the head close to his ear and exclaimed, "You even have a phone in the bathtub!" He was not joking. Two generations younger than my great-uncle, and according-ly more comfortable with all the gadgets that *improve* our lives these days, I've come to appreciate the convenience of picking up a phone to be instantly connected with anyone, anywhere, anytime. But I remember well my childhood when the phone was a luxury used always with restraint, mostly for special and usually bad news. My heart still jumps a little each time the ringing interrupts our routine. It jumps a lot when the phone rings at night.

So I left our bed that night with trepidation at the jin-gling intrusion.

"Chris?" Mom's voice was so distant and controlled I hardly recognized it. "There are people in the back yard."

With a quick breath I reached for an explanation. "Gosh, are the neighborhood kids having a party?"

"I don't know but I see them."

Halloween had come and gone, and on that cold Novem-ber night with new snow hanging from roofs and branches, I couldn't imagine children merrily chasing each other, or a ball, into Mom's yard. "Hmmm. Are they close to the fence? Maybe they are looking for something?"

"I don't know. I hear them laughing and I don't want them in the yard."

"Oh, right. They shouldn't be there. Are they coming closer or causing trouble?"

"I don't think so."

"I wonder if they're having a party and just fooling around. Maybe they're having a scavenger hunt and will leave soon?"

"Yes, that must be it."

Remarkable, isn't it, how in dire circumstances, people will agree to accept as reasonable what under normal condi-tions they would think ludicrous. On some level Mom and I both knew that this was not a night for children to be playing outside, but we followed the rules of the game of make-believe to which we had unwittingly consented. Still, such pretense took its toll and Mom, obviously unconvinced by our manufactured explanation, sounded drained by her effort to cross the gulf between her equally impossible *and* real perceptions.

"I think I'll go back to bed."

"Good idea, Mom! Keep your curtains and doors tightly closed and try to ignore them. Curtis should be home soon."

"OK. Good night."

Mom hung up almost before I could finish, "Good night to you, too, Mom. And call back if you feel there is any trouble."

Having heard only my half of the conversation, Paul greeted me with questioning eyes. I crawled back into bed searching for the words to describe the conversation Mom and I had just had. I could not explain to him what I couldn't fathom myself. Then, and not for the first time, I regretted having honored Mom's request not to get her another dog when our last pet had died. Dancer was a Yellow Lab mix, all legs and tongue and love, who would not be ignored. Even if only her rump was heavily leaning against your legs as she nonchalantly edged herself into the scene, she was a constant and reassuring presence. She was my best running buddy; and Mom and I cried unashamedly when the veterinarian ended her suffering from pancreatic cancer by "putting her to sleep" while her head with trusting eyes open rested calmly on Mom's foot.

I well understood Mom's insistence that, nearing eighty, she did not want another dog. Leaving it would simply be too hard. Mom knew that sooner or later she would either outlive or be outlived by another beloved pet. She didn't want to put herself through another of those wrenching good-byes. But how helpful a Dancer would be now! Wistfully, I imagined her efficiently dispersing kids or deer or any other intruder the minute Mom released her into the backyard. Without malice, but claiming total right-of-place, Dancer would have restored order out there in no time.

Restoring order in Mom's mind, of course, was an entirely different matter. Paul and I remembered at the same time that there really had been no dog in the bay in Maine. What could Mom possibly have seen as people in her backyard now? The snowy night left us with more questions than answers as, half an hour later, the phone rang again.

"They are still out there. I think they need a place to sleep. I see their sleeping bags."

Dear God, what do I say?

But Mom went on, "I don't want them in my yard..." and provided me with an opening, "Oh no, Mom, of course not! No one should sleep in your yard."

"But what if they don't have a place to stay?"

"Well, Boulder has a good homeless shelter and everyone has a warm place to sleep tonight." As I was in my nightgown, and even dressed would have had no idea how I would handle this if Mom agreed, I halfheartedly added: "Should I come over and talk with them?"

"No. Curtis will be home soon. And if they don't go away I'll call the police."

That was a new twist. I couldn't recall our family ever having sought police intervention. But at that moment Mom seemed reassured by this potential source of help. She agreed to go back to bed and let whatever was going on in the outside world continue.

One of the many healthful attributes I inherited from the Vagt side of the family is an ability to sleep through storms that keep others awake. Following what had been a restless night for everyone else, I would crawl out of bed many a morning to an exasperated chorus of, "You'd sleep through being carried from a burning house." To be fair, they were right. I am a very sound sleeper. In the late 1960s, we spent a summer in Scranton, Pennsylvania. Dad had a teaching position at a Jesuit university there, and for ten weeks we lived in a beautiful old house right on the main street. My bedroom not only looked out on a busy street, but its large bay window extended closer to the noisy traffic than the bedroom windows at the back of the house. I nevertheless always slept through the night.

Even the night a drunk driver slammed into a power pole sending it crashing down onto our property. With sirens wailing and lights flashing, the rescue workers hauled the unhurt driver to jail. The utility crew worked through the night removing the splintered pole and securing downed wires to assure safe passage through the neighborhood for the morning rush hour. I slept through it all, waking with astonishment to the mayhem in front of our house. My smiling parents shook their heads in disbelief as they described the night's events to me. I felt thoroughly deprived at the time, but as an adult appreciate the ability to get a good night's sleep as a gift.

I slept through the night of Mom's uninvited guests, too. But morning came early and I was anxious to head across town to see just what had happened the night before at her house. I wasn't surprised, I think, but crestfallen at the sight of the smooth layer of snow sparkling in the morning sun across Mom's lawn—undisturbed by footprints of night visitors. We had been pretty sure that no group of homeless folks had set up camp in Mom's back yard. I had, however, hoped that deer, a family of raccoons, or even a neighbor's dog had caused the confusion and left their tracks as evidence.

"Good morning, dear Mom, how are you feeling?" I announced my arrival cheerily before entering her house. Mom gamely assured me she was fine, though tired, her face betraying an anxious, sleepless night. I was reluctant to bring up the subject of the previous night's phone calls. It wouldn't do to remind her of the unpleasant experience. Later in Mom's disease process, she would forget about her visitors, those she alone would meet in her confusion and those who would sign into the guest book at Mountainview, within moments of their leaving. But at that time, there was no way either of us had been able to forget the stress of the night. So I casually risked inquiring whether she'd had any more trouble with the "people" in her yard.

"Yes, I didn't want them to stay around so I called the police."

I was amazed that amid the muddle of Mom's thinking, she had sorted out the details for contacting the police. Maybe she just knew to dial 9-1-1? I would get in touch with them later, ask them to check their records, and try to learn what had actually happened. For the moment I was grateful Mom had pursued a solution.

"Good, Mom! Were they helpful?"

She said the two officers had been "very nice," but unfortunately not very effective. Apparently they couldn't find the "people." They did promise to drive through the neighborhood throughout the night to keep an eye on the house and assured Mom that whoever disturbed her must have gone home. They also encouraged her to call again if she saw anything unusual or felt she needed help. When Paul and I checked the police records the next day, we learned that Mom had done exactly that, twice. According to the incident report, neither officer found any evidence of intruders, but they responded to each call with a visit and genuine efforts to reassure the caller: my poor Mom.

The last call registered in the police log came about 10:45 p.m. I heard later from Curtis that he had arrived home from his volleyball game about eleven to find his Omi dressed and wandering through his part of the house. Staunch respecters of each other's privacy throughout the years of their shared living arrangement, Curtis was startled to be greeted by anyone, especially his Omi, upon his return. This had never happened before; something was terribly wrong. Mom was still distressed, but had calmed down the minute she saw her tall, handsome grandson entering the house. As she explained what she had seen, Curtis grew curious. He checked doors and windows, the garage access and back porch to find only undisturbed snow in a silent night. Agreeing that whoever had been out and about earlier had by then left, they both retired to a rest neither believed they'd get, but desperately needed.

Although she made no effort to be hospitable, the "people" obviously liked Mom's back yard. They returned regularly, day and night, and I began to hate them. When I called from work to say that I was just about to leave the office and would meet Mom for coffee, *they* were "just outside." When I arrived and inspected the area for evidence of visitors, *they* were lurking down by the fence. And when I searched Mom's small yard to chase them off, I found no one. All the while, though, *they* remained visible to Mom.

"I see them underneath that big tree over there," Mom would gesture vaguely in the direction of the large blue spruce. But in the time it took me to get to where I thought she was pointing, the "people" had disappeared and again successfully evaded my efforts to evict them. We all grew weary of their cunning, and Mom stopped asking Curtis and me to chase them off. She didn't think we could really help since, as she explained, "*They* always hide from you and Curtis." To her they remained clear and present.

The next Sunday at church I confided in a friend, a registered nurse, who had endured her own mother's aging in a nursing home. I asked her for an explanation as a friend and a professional.

"What on Earth might be going on with Mom?" Mostly to convince myself, I assured her, "There simply were no people in her yard, and no wild animals, pets, or snow-laden trees to be mistaken for people either!" Not willing to write Mom off as delusional, however, I quickly added, "But there's no question that Mom saw them plainly."

My friend responded by putting her arms around me, whispering, "Oh Chris, I'm so sorry it has begun."

I didn't know exactly what *it* was and couldn't muster the courage to ask, but I'd heard and read just enough about dementia in the elderly to be terrified by where this turn in our mother-daughter journey might be taking us.

Off the Path: Early 2003

*"It is advisable that a person know at least three things:
where they are, where they are going, and what they had best do
under the circumstances."*
– John Ruskin

MOM'S DECADES OF careful planning had spoiled me for ever coping well with not knowing either where we were, where we were going, or for that matter, what we had best do in that situation. It then dawned on me that Mom and I had been batting zero on all three counts, and that wouldn't do. Even if I was pretty sure I wouldn't like what I'd learn from more research about aging and dementia, I needed more information; so Mom and I were off again to see her physician. We learned that very rarely the Wellbutrin Mom was taking daily *can* induce hallucinations. But I was impatient with playing the odds of possibility and analyzing history. We'd been through that, and whatever else the antidepressants might have done to or for her, so far there'd been only a noticeable worsening of Mom's condition. None of us any longer believed the initial diagnosis of depression, and I insisted there must be a more aggressive approach we could pursue to relieve Mom's distress—regardless of what we called it!

I perked up when the doctor mentioned the anti-psychotic drugs available for the elderly. Reluctantly, my hopes rose further when I heard from several different sources that the Resperadol Mom's doctor next prescribed for her was indeed a "very good drug." A colleague at the University even confided that her father-in-law had recently started taking it and showed almost immediate improvement. We started Mom on the same medication and saw the same results. Within a month or so of their arrival, the "people" had left Mom's yard for good.

We couldn't say that the visitors had fully left her mind, or whether Mom just decided to stop mentioning their appearance. With Mom's curtains to her beloved back patio closed more frequently, and Mom rarely leaving the house now, it was hard to tell. What we could see was that when the "people" arrived they were real and present to her. After all, she saw them, and we all know that our eyes don't lie. But as soon as the dementia subsided, Mom knew just as clearly that Curtis and I couldn't see her visitors, and worse, we could not protect her from their coming or make them go away. How do you hide from something that inhabits your mind? Occasionally, Mom's eyes would relax while recalling my reaction to something she had told me earlier: "I could tell by your face you didn't believe me," she'd tease. "Was I talking nonsense again?" In response I'd hug her with relief, grateful for her ability to retain her courage and humor. More often, though, she'd just retreat deeper into that oppressive silence that's all that remains when there is no longer common ground between two people. Though we were standing close together, and holding hands tightly everywhere we walked, Mom was nevertheless slipping away from me, steadily retreating into a world where I could not follow.

Mornings were usually easier. When I would call Mom from my office to say good-morning, it would be obvious that we'd started the day in broadly the same universe. By mid-morning she would become tired, though, returning to bed for "a little rest." Mom always felt "comfy-cozy" in her bed and thankfully did so for the rest of her life. But once she had risen from her afternoon nap, and certainly by the time I had arrived for our after-work cup of decaf, her mind was in what we came to call a *jumble*. I would learn that this confused restlessness is common in individuals suffering with dementia, and is casually referred to as "Sundowner's Effect" for generally occurring in the late afternoon or early evening. At the time I only knew that although the symptoms might vary from day to day, if I got to Mom's house later than four in the afternoon, her perceptions were hopelessly *jumbled.*

What didn't change was that the themes of her "Sundowner's" would consistently revolve around her life-long occupation of homemaking and caring for her family. Several times she was adamant that, though exhausted, she could not possibly lie down to rest again. She had heard her grandson Mike knocking at the door, while Curtis, inexplicably, had refused to let him in. "I don't understand why Curtis wouldn't open the door, but I have to stay up to let Mike in," she agonized.

Other times, as I hugged her upon my arrival, Mom's eyes would search behind me, not exactly unhappy to see me, but clearly waiting for someone else. "Are all the people who slept downstairs with you? They left before I could give them their breakfast," she confessed. Pretty certain no one had slept downstairs, I felt ridiculous, but nevertheless tried to reassure Mom by offering an excuse for their absence. "Maybe they went out to eat?" At which point Mom began to worry that she didn't know when they'd be back. Going downstairs together to find no unmade beds or suitcases in Mom's neat guestroom did nothing to ease her dismay at not having properly provided for her visiting family.

Grasping at any comfort, I counted as a slight improvement the fact that at least the uninvited guests were no longer strangers. It must be less stressful for her, I reasoned, to have family come to visit. But reason had passed out of reach and in my effort to calm Mom, one after another my explanations failed.

"Maybe you had a dream during your nap about Christmas vacation when Ute was here? You don't need to worry about that anymore. Everyone is back home now and well cared for."

That only offended Mom. Why would I suggest that she couldn't tell the difference between a dream and folks staying in her guestroom? She did admit to not remembering *exactly* who had spent the night with her, but beyond that neither of us could think of anything else to say.

I also couldn't decide whether it was better to call Mom

before I left the office to prepare her for my arrival, or whether the anticipation would just make things worse. It could go either way. But while my hope never waned that my afternoon visits offered Mom a toehold on reality my belief that I could pull Mom out of her *jumble* with my mere presence was weakening. Although we'd agreed years before that a piece of pastry from the best French bakery in town was too pricey for all but special occasions, Mom would now insist almost daily that I stop at "that good place and bring some baked stuff." She'd pay me back of course, as soon as I had arrived. Her "bring us some nice pieces" expressed Mom's enduring hope that an afternoon sweet could corral our rapidly escaping sense of sanity and reclaim comforts of the past. Who was I to deny my Mom one of her few remaining pleasures—and only dream? I would swing by the shop for three (one for Curtis, too) fancy pastries.

Ever the hostess, Mom would greet me at the door. But the minute she noticed the small box in my hand, frustration fell across her face like a shadow. As soon as I stepped into her house I understood why. Neatly laid out on her table would be perhaps ten full sets of after-dinner ware: dessert plates and forks, cups and saucers, napkins, a sugar bowl and silver milk pitcher. Two huge carafes filled with hot, fresh-brewed coffee would sit on the counter, with all the chairs Mom owned arranged around her coffee tables. Mom would be expecting lots of company and my paltry contribution would hardly be sufficient.

To my questions about the elaborate set-up, Mom would respond, "I talked to them on the phone this afternoon. I'm sure everybody is coming." I've yet to learn who *everybody* was. Mom couldn't remember and I never knew. I do know that they never showed up, their rudeness resulting in many cups of coffee being poured down the sink and expensive cream and custard pastries going stale.

Throughout those winter months, two unshakable perceptions settled in Mom's mind and marked her disease from then on. Somehow, in Mom's world, it was always Sunday—the traditional day for family gatherings and large meals. And the awaited guests were always polite enough to call ahead. That way Mom could know to expect them and prepare for their arrival. Sometimes I still try to figure out if these misperceptions were the cause or the result of her confusion. Did she really *hear* the voices on the phone suggesting her guests' visit? Or did the sameness of her days in social isolation, lacking any work schedule or appointments, lead her simply to conclude that it must be that quietest of days, Sunday, when family traditionally came to call? Which *did* come first, the chicken or the egg?

It wouldn't matter, of course, except that I tried for weeks to find ways to level out Mom's wildly fluctuating perceptions. Or more accurately, it seemed ever more important for me to try to forestall her increasing disappointment as Mom's joyous anticipation of her visitors quickly collapsed in a huge letdown and cruel reminder of her failing health.

"Hi Mom," I would try on the phone, "I just wanted you to know that I'm still at my office. As soon as I finish here at work I'll be over for my visit. But since it's a work day, I think I'm probably the only one who can make it today."

Mom always thanked me for calling and said how good it would be to see me. But my call did nothing to ground her in my reality for long. Fifteen minutes later I'd arrive to see the same expectant gaze, the house prepared for guests, "Are the others coming behind you?"

"Gosh, I'm not sure anyone else can make it today; it will be just the two of us."

"But my Mum called and said she'd come for a visit on Sunday."

"Well, maybe Sunday. But today is only Wednesday."

She would be incredulous. "Really?" To her credit, recognizing her mistake would reliably make Mom laugh. "I always think it's Sunday, don't I?"

"That's okay, Mom. Sunday's a nice day," I said before taking her hand. Swinging our arms in rhythm we'd then walk over to her couch singing that great gospel hymn, "Ev'ry day'll be Sunday by and by... by and by." It did not escape my notice that the gospel vision of all those lovely Sundays referred to somewhere not in this life. But as long as Mom and I were in tune together, fine points of theology seemed irrelevant.

Besides, relaxed moments were brief as our singing was almost immediately followed by a crushing let down. "I think you're right; it's getting dark now and I don't think anybody's coming any more today."

Sometimes Mom would reluctantly let me help her put all the plates and cups and saucers back into the cupboards. Angry with I don't know whom with each disappointment Mom had to suffer, I would unceremoniously dump the still-steaming coffee into the sink. The milk in the silver pitchers would stay on the counter, "…in case they still come by I want to have something ready." Letting milk go sour seemed a small price to pay for Mom's hopes.

The real cost of those fruitless preparations, of course, was significantly higher. Mom would wear herself out hauling the furniture into place and, absorbed in the process, she'd either forget to eat her lunch altogether or, more frequently, snack all day on the sweet leftovers from yesterday's no-shows. I tried to redirect the pattern of Mom's thinking by focusing on the quiet visit *just the two of us* will have that afternoon, and suggest, "I'll bring some fresh fruit or yogurt for a snack for us."

Suddenly, Mom was concerned about waste. "Oh no! I don't need any of *that* stuff," she would object vehemently. "I won't be able to pack that. It'll just go bad."

Good Lord! My mind whirled in a tailspin trying to figure out where Mom was and where we could be going. It obviously required luggage. With no guidance, divine or otherwise, I simply chose to arrive with strawberries and milk, a real treat I fondly remembered Mom fixing for us as children. Ute and I especially loved drinking the sweet milk stained pink from our halving the strawberries with our spoons before eating them. Would Mom remember those good moments? Her annoyance at my purchase provided the answer. Why had I brought something she couldn't take to her "other house," she asked?

84

OVER THE YEARS of Mom's increasingly erratic behavior, I liked to believe that I was getting better at maintaining my mental equilibrium—no matter what. Unconsciously I had somehow adjusted enough to the effects of Mom's illness to at least tolerate, if not yet expect, the unexpected. But that was a new one. "*What* other house?" I thought frantically to myself. I decided to sidestep Mom's comment. "Well, if we don't finish all the strawberries and milk we can just stick them in the fridge here, don't you think?"

"Okay, if you think so." My solution didn't make enough sense to Mom for her to wholeheartedly agree, but weary and confused, she couldn't muster enough of her own reality to counter mine. While we were enjoying the fruit, Mom looked around with the wonder of someone surveying a place she'd never seen before. "And who is taking care of the bills at my house?"

"We are, Mom. You and I do your checkbook here every month."

"Yes, I know we do that for HERE—but what about *at home?*"

I wanted to run away. As fast as my legs could carry me, I wanted to get away from whatever was keeping my poor Mom from recognizing the living room she had loved for over twenty years. Only Mom's pleading eyes held me back, imploring mine for an explanation I didn't have. Somewhere along the way I'd learned that asking more questions is a good substitute for providing an answer. "Don't you feel like you're at home here?"

Mom kept searching, willing her brain to recognize her surroundings. "That *is* my piano over there, isn't it?"

"Right!" I even startled myself as I shouted at the opportunity to step out of the muck and back onto familiar and common ground. "And you always say you are so comfortable on that couch."

"Yes, that is true, isn't it?" Her brow furrowed. She was still unsure. But the worst had passed, though not without exhausting us both with the effort to maintain some semblance of normalcy. When I called Mom later that evening she was already in bed. She said she was puzzled though. Since she hadn't done anything all day she couldn't imagine why she should be so tired. When I told her that I was already in my *jammies* too, she did grant that at some stages of life, merely surviving is sufficiently grueling work to exhaust one.

I hoped it also justified my tears flowing ever more frequently. To trade war stories and process our experiences with Mom, Curtis and I were meeting regularly for lunch. We badly needed to confirm our sanity in light of some of the unbelievable conversations we were having with her. During one particularly weepy moment, Curtis gave me what would become my mantra for the rest of the journey. "It'll never make sense, Mom. Just *cover the moment!*"

I think it's fair to say that Curtis is more laid-back than I am and I don't use that term in a pejorative sense. Curtis could get so intensely and passionately involved in an art project, for example, that he would forget to eat for a whole day or more. But when it comes to the routine details of the day, he takes a big-picture view. That allows him to sail unperturbed past those minutiae that upset me when they don't go as planned. He did not inherit his grandmother's need for supreme order. Or maybe he decided early on that his mother and grandmother had done enough planning for all three lifetimes. In either case, he takes a far more relaxed approach to the future and consequently rides out life's invariable bumps and missed connections more easily than Mom and I could. Learning from him has served me well. For Mom there were no more plans to be made, and no future to look toward. And thankfully, there were ever fewer sad or upsetting memories to haunt her present. There was only *this* moment for us to share whatever perceptions rose from the murky associations in Mom's mind—and to "cover it."

Most of Mom's physical movement was now limited to her house and her immediate surroundings. Always the mother at heart, she still wanted to carry the tray with coffee and cookies to me, and when I was ready to head home she always got up and walked around the garage to see me to my car. Going there we would hold hands, but once I was driving away, I knew she was on her own and I worried. I was scared she'd fall because the strength and independence that used to get her wherever she wanted to go had been replaced by a tentative, fearful shuffle. Often, even while just getting up to go to the bathroom, Mom would mention that she felt like she was floating when she walked. Her concern that, "My legs just don't go where I want them to," was a good enough reason for her not to leave the house. We were relieved that she didn't want to venture forth anymore. But it was spring again, and there was that elephant in the room with us. For weeks we managed to politely ignore it—until one afternoon Mom broke our conspiracy of silence and announced that she didn't think she had the strength to go with me to Maine *this year*.

I knew Mom was absolutely right. Even my optimism was overcome by the relentless onslaught of reality. I had been wondering how on earth we would get through the endless hours and miles of the trip east. But I was enough of my father's daughter to be content ignoring the obvious as long as possible, to then be genuinely shattered by Mom's accurate assessment.

Unwilling to give in, I persisted. "How about trying the doctor one more time? Just to make sure they're doing all they can to help you feel better?" Mom was nothing if not a good sport, and we followed her physician's suggestion to explore several more things before throwing in the towel on our Maine summer.

First, we went to a physical therapist for that unsteady leg-swing that now passed for Mom's walk. The session was relatively short and we left with an exercise band (soon banned to the garage) and with confirmation of what we already knew. Mom's muscles were strong. She responded to every stimulus with the same determination she'd brought to handling all of life, and her arms and legs worked just fine. What was not cooperating was her brain. As I had noticed for the first time in the hotel bathroom a year earlier, Mom's brain didn't seem to be sending the correct messages either about where her feet were or the mechanics of how to propel them forward. It was possible that she had suffered a minor stroke, or was in fact still having an occasional TIA. (Transient Ischemic Attacks are temporary intermittent neurological events also known as mini-strokes.)

Our next appointment was at the Kaiser facility in Denver for an MRI brain scan.[11] The forty-five minute drive, with Mom worried and disoriented next to me, seemed interminable. Once we left the highway, Mom found somewhere to focus her anxious energy: street signs. She counted out loud every one of the many blocks we were driving to our destination. Triumphantly she announced with all seriousness, "Here's 111th, this is 112th," as if she were imparting new and important information with each intersection. "Now we're at 113th, 114th, 115th, etc." I tried to contain the nagging irritation that rose with each recited number and settled on gloom instead. What chaos was compelling Mom to grasp for order in that sound of tiny, sequential pieces of information? She had no idea where we were. But even after we had arrived and checked in at the hospital Mom was only mildly nervous as they slid her under the MRI gantry. The ordeal was over before we fully realized it had begun. The doctor's follow-up call to report the findings was equally anti-climactic. There was no evidence of brain damage and Mom should probably visit a neuropsychologist for a more comprehensive evaluation of her functional impairment.

After one more drive to Denver we arrived at yet another doctor's office. Again holding hands, we followed the nurse's directions to the examining room. Trying to put us at ease, the doctor asked about Mom's accent, which has remained noticeable throughout her forty years in this country, but was then unmistakably increased by her nervousness. We talked casually about our beginnings in a very different place. He asked where in Germany we were from, and what had brought us here. As we engaged in friendly chit-chat, without warning, the doctor asked, "Do you know where you are now?" His approach could have been interpreted as a smooth transition. But Mom, who had been participating freely in the conversation until

---

11   Magnetic Resonance Imaging uses the properties of magnetism to create nondestructive, three-dimensional, internal images of the soft tissues of the body, including brain, spinal cord and muscle.

then, couldn't keep up. She stared at him in uncomprehending silence. Frankly, I was a little taken aback, too.

"Hey wait," my mind turned defensively on the doctor, "we never decided where the *here* of our banter was. Be a little precise, man! Do you want to know whether Mom knows she's no longer in Germany? Or are you trying to discern whether Mom's aware that we just spent an hour driving from Boulder to Denver?"

Mom took a deep breath reaching for an answer, but remained silent. I wanted to jump in and save her the embarrassment of having to explain to a stranger that she knew Hamburg, Altona and Dassendorf. She could distinguish between Boulder and Denver, for that matter, if only he'd be a bit more explicit with his question. When Mom finally uttered Boulder (as opposed to Germany, mind you!) rather than Denver, I took her hand and smiled approval. I was hoping my gesture reassured her without betraying how much I despised both the medical process and the dire prognosis, which I knew would be made after we had gone.

I watched as the doctor duly noted that Mom did not know where she was before he proceeded with a few more questions. "Do you know what year it is?"

Mom had no idea, but did it really matter? I seethed inside.

"Do you know who the President is?" The doctor even added the hint that a few years ago his father had also been President. Given her own experience of being a citizen of a nation of hostile aggressors in the late 1930s and of losing seventeen of her own family in one night's Allied fire-bombing raid on Hamburg, there was little Mom feared and despised more than war and the men who try to justify it. That she could not remember that George W. Bush was our president was inconceivable to me. But Mom's memory, by then totally overwhelmed, failed her on everything and her eyes went vacant. And there we went again with the three familiar categories: food, car, color, followed by the watch face. This time Mom's drawing resembled an indecipherable scribble of numbers bunched into the first quarter of a squiggly oval. At this telling

failure, my mind returned to the doctor's congratulatory explanation for the perfectly round and legible watch set at 10:20
she had drawn less than two years earlier. I felt myself becoming enraged at the obvious. "You always *know* what time it is,"
I wanted to scream. "How could you have caught a lifetime of
buses, always on schedule, if you couldn't recognize a watch?
And further, you know damn well who is President. Don't you
remember how often you muted the television news about the
Congressional votes and speeches supporting the U.S. invasion of Iraq? I know you *know* these things!"

But Mom didn't. While I could barely contain my anger
with the doctor for exposing Mom's confusion, or, probably
more accurately, for undermining my well-practiced pretense,
Mom smiled politely and hand in hand we fled the place of her
ruin. The doctor stayed behind to make the few notations that
I learned later had become permanently inscribed on Mom's
medical records: *Severe memory loss.*

"NO kidding!" is all I could offer in acid response to the
nurse calling to report the findings. I wasn't trying to be disrespectful of the doctors and the medical facility. Everyone
was kind and professional. The anger and sadness at the
day's unremarkable diagnosis were my problem and not of
their making.

MAY OF THAT year brought two notable events: Curtis was
awarded his Master of Fine Arts degree from Naropa University, and a few days later I purchased a single airline ticket
for Maine. They are related only in that Curtis's graduation
convinced even my unwilling mind that Mom was right when
she judged that *this* year she wasn't well enough to travel east
with me. We never discussed whether she actually believed she
could make the trip the following year, but taking this bitter
medicine gradually made it a little easier to swallow. Regardless, that experience of late May was another eye-opener for
eyes I could have sworn were already wide open.

Following a warm, dry spring, on the day before Curtis's graduation the skies dumped a foot and a half of snow on the Front Range. Outdoor commencement ceremonies were canceled all across the state as a foot and a half of heavy, wet flakes blanketed the area. Such spring storms are not unheard of in Colorado, but many of the larger institutions did not have an inside venue large enough to accommodate their graduation exercises. Those of us with Naropa graduates were fortunate. The relatively small size of their graduating class allowed Naropa to schedule its ceremonies for Macky Auditorium. One of the beautiful, old buildings on the University of Colorado campus, it was a fitting place to celebrate Curtis's achievement. He continued the tradition begun with his grandfather's professorship and the awarding of my own Master's degree there a decade earlier. Curtis was his own man who had chosen his own path, but I felt immensely proud to be slowly trudging hand in hand with Mom through this snowy campus toward his graduation.

Mom was game for it, and although she obviously had little idea where we were or why we were struggling with such treacherous footing, she plodded along. Once inside the festively decorated but crushingly crowded auditorium, however, she became increasingly agitated. For a while I worried whether it had been a mistake to bring her, but my fears evaporated the minute she saw Curtis march across the stage to receive his diploma. Instantly, Mom's face relaxed and lit up with the recognition of her beloved grandson—the effort had been worth it after all!

Still, in order to beat the crowds after the ceremony, I decided to usher Mom out a little early. We still had a few preparations to finish for the celebratory dinner gathering at our house, and I wasn't disappointed to miss the mass exodus either. We stepped from the dark auditorium into a bright, sunny day. Colorado had reasserted its springtime identity. In a few hours the skies had moved effortlessly between winter and summer. But it took the ground a little longer to melt the mounds of snow from the storm. Roads and paths were still a mess of slippery slush. Even able-footed folks who would have easily walked across campus under normal circumstances were being picked up close to the auditorium to avoid the difficult footing. There was no question that Paul would do the same for Mom. He walked ahead to retrieve our car and picked us up right at the bottom of the stairs.

Mom and I had only a few steps to take outside, and yet the effort was so wearying for her that the truth about the approaching summer landed on me like the proverbial ton of bricks. For the moment, I had other things to think about. I ignored Mom's clutching my arm for much more than physical stability against the wet ground during her unsteady walk to the car. Family and friends, including Curtis's father and grandparents, were joining in his day of honor at our house. For those of us with memory, the day was memorable, indeed. Mom, however, could no longer recall any part of either this event or its meaning for Curtis's life. When she asked later whether Curtis was in school, she wasn't asking about his teaching or graduate work, but about the little boy she used to send off to elementary school. "Does Curtis have anything to eat? I didn't make him his lunch today."

Curtis's graduation proved a rite of passage for me, too. The die had been cast. I couldn't fathom how I could make it to Maine with Mom. Yet I couldn't imagine going without her either. I despised both Mom's disease and her forthrightness as she maintained that just *this* year I had better go on our summer vacation without her. With that mischievous flicker in her eyes (so familiar, but so rare those days), she even added, "It's about time you and Paul have a honeymoon without the mother-in-law in tow."

Momentarily able to revert to her role as adult, she was right both about her abilities and about Paul and I needing some time alone. So, I set about making arrangements for my three-week absence from her. I began at the Boulder County Aging Services Division office and a visit with a Community Care Coordinator. In addition to providing me with badly needed emotional support, the counselors had much information to help meet my practical needs for Mom. The Boulder Valley has a number of options for in-home elder care, from skilled nurses to professional care services and volunteer companions. Over the next weeks we explored all types of services. Realizing that it would take time for Mom to accept such interventions, we tried several approaches. They failed one after another.

Not only did they not work for Mom, they made things worse. Whether it was the nurse or the "Friendly Visitor," Mom couldn't relax knowing someone was coming by to see her. Still wanting to be a good hostess, she felt the urgent need to prepare, offer, serve, clean—to be in charge. As one being cared for, she did not cope well with the repeated reminders of her new role as the one unable to complete what used to be routine tasks. Mom would not allow anyone to do anything for her: neither the purely practical shopping or housecleaning, nor the more personal conversations on the back patio. If, on the other hand, I didn't remind her that on that day her companion was coming, or she forgot it minutes thereafter, she'd be upset that someone had arrived unannounced. Irritated at both the surprise and the intrusion, Mom would challenge, "But what do they want here?" And regardless of how often I tried to explain that they would just like to spend a little time with her, she rejected them outright. When I suggested they could vacuum or take her shopping, all tasks I was by then doing for Mom and could definitely have used help with, she resisted with, "No! I was going to do that tomorrow." Tomorrow, of course, never came, and I gave up when Mom rejected even going on a short drive into the mountains with one of her caregivers, explaining that, "I've already been up there."

I was shattered by her words and utterly confused by the unfamiliar person inhabiting Mom's body. This couldn't be my Mom; she was no longer happily planning and anticipating the next outing. "Mom," my mind was in turmoil, "don't you remember? We can take the same trip a thousand times but *it always looks different!*" She did not remember and I quietly swallowed my fury.

Lost: Early Fall 2003

"Whether you say you can, or say you can't, you are right."
–Henry Ford

I MAY HAVE purchased my ticket for Maine, but as things stood, I saw no way I could leave Colorado for a vacation. Frustration turned everything I did and thought to sadness. Thankfully, just before I was forced to admit defeat by that formidable foe of Mom's illness, Ute jumped to the rescue. During one of our frequent conversations while Ute listened and I vented, she offered to spend one of her summer vacation months in Colorado. She had wanted to help more all along and made me feel even better by insisting that, anyway, she had long wished to have more time with Mom. Ute suggested she could drive rather than fly the thousand-plus miles from her Oregon home. She could thereby keep the length of her stay open and, no less important, bring her beloved dog, Winston. Mom's place was comfortable for one, but would be small for two adults and a big dog. So that the three of them would not be constantly on top of each other, Ute and Winston would stay at our place to housesit. From there they could enjoy Boulder's pleasant lifestyle and natural beauty while Paul and I were in Maine. But most of all, Ute would give me a break while experiencing firsthand the privilege and burden of walking with Mom through the deepening canyons of her decline.

It was the perfect solution for all. Ute and Mom regained an appreciation for one another that decades of distance had eroded. Ute and I learned something of the guilt and jealousies that had driven two loving but very different sisters apart, and about the forgiveness and understanding required to heal the rift. As a couple for the first time in years, Paul and I took excursions into the Canadian Maritimes we could never have taken with Mom. We especially loved discovering Prince Edward Island, swimming in the Gulf of St. Lawrence, and sharing an intimacy difficult to pursue while Mom slept nearby. For his part, Winston was one happy pup poking his head, right up to his shoulders, through the railing of our front deck in Boulder, surveying his domain from that lofty perch overlooking the Flatirons.

Throughout the three-week vacation, I only lost my composure once—right at the start. Standing on the moving walkway underneath the colorful streams of light along the inter-concourse tunnels at O'Hare airport, I suddenly missed terribly the happy anticipation Mom and I would share while changing planes on the way to Maine. Surrounded by thousands of people going to their various destinations, I felt utterly alone, knowing Mom and I would never pass there on our way to *Paradise* together again. For as we know now (and did then), it was not just *that* year that Mom couldn't make the trip to Maine. In its stead, Ute's summer visit to Colorado became an annual event solidifying our sisterly partnership and strengthening the whole family around Mom.

After three marvelous weeks *off*, part of me dreaded going home. Who doesn't prefer the careless days of vacation over the grind of daily life—especially one I feared would never again be *normal* as we'd known it. But I had also genuinely missed Mom. I was spoiled, I know, to be over fifty and still find her strength and self-effacing wit a present, if ever more rare, resource. At least I returned refreshed by sea air and Paul's love. Ute's greater understanding of Mom's distress and her commitment to participate in easing it were also a comfort. So once Ute took to the long western road back to her coast, I threw myself into helping Mom with renewed energy.

Maybe as some evidence that Mom's world really was topsy-turvy, Ute had saved Mom's messages to *me* on our home phone. The tape was filled with short, informational calls from her saying how nice it was that Ute had come to visit that day, and inquiring, "When you come over to see me, please stop at

96

the bakery for something nice to eat."

Ute returned home to a similar set of voice recordings from Mom trying to reach her in Oregon. It was heartbreaking to realize that Mom had had no idea where to find either of us. In spite of the large-type "summer" phone list I had left for her, she had never once dialed the Maine number to reach me, or our home number in Boulder to reach Ute. If born in hopelessness, it was nevertheless somewhat comforting to realize that Mom apparently never quite understood that I had been in Maine. Although I had called her from there daily and told her how much we missed her, she never knew where I was—or what she was missing. Mom had not been sitting in Boulder pining away for *Paradise* or even fully realizing her other losses. Mom couldn't remember them! And with that, I thought I might be catching a glimpse of that tiniest of gifts that the forgetting mind bestows.

THE EMOTIONAL RESPITE from that revelation was short-lived, however. What the forgetting actually inflicted on Mom was the cruel and relentless uncertainty that arises when every thought and decision has only the present moment to draw upon as a reference. Having to choose a path of action with no experiential or historical referent must be terrifying for the one with severe memory loss! The afflicted's repetitive behaviors, while they clutch at veiled, vaguely recognizable clues, can be almost intolerable for those loving them. Everyone's expression of dementia and memory loss is unique to that individual, and for Mom it always revolved around her wish to be with her family, especially to connect across time with her parents. Although I had gotten into the habit of calling Mom at least twice a day before visiting her, it was not unusual for me to return home at the end of the day to five, seven, ten phone messages from Mom on our machine. With each call her voice would sound different—stiffly formal some times, extremely agitated at others—but with no indication that Mom knew she had called moments earlier with the same question, "Hello Chris, I'm trying to reach my Mum, do you have her number?" Or, "This is your mother calling. Did you hear from my Mum?" Then, "I need to find my Mum's phone number." Followed by, "Call me back right away, please, to let me know whether you called my Mum."

When Mom first started expecting her parents to visit, I would say that since they were in Germany, I really thought they had too far to travel to stop by for afternoon coffee. Once she had lost all sense of geographic distances, I hoped to reroute some of her yearning by reminding her that many of our family in Germany were by then deceased. Passing quickly from the weight of that message, I could then easily get Mom to talk about her Mum by mentioning that I had been only five when my grandmother died, and would love to be told more about her. But by the time Mom was sending those frantic phone messages, those early tricks weren't working anymore and I changed tactics again. I could not, would not lie to her, and found a way to keep my commitment to tell Mom "The Truth" by reminding her that we could, unfortunately, not reach her parents. They did not, after all, have a telephone or even electricity in Dassendorf. So we just had to trust that they were well where they were. That explanation would help Mom momentarily relax, even though often she would have no recollection of her continued requests for their number. As if my mentioning that her parents were in Dassendorf was simply my thoughtfulness, she'd thank me profusely for the reminder. We'd end the conversation with, "Good night, sleep tight." Then, at the very last moment before hanging up, tacked on like a brand-new afterthought, Mom would catch her breath and add, "Oh, I meant to ask, do you have my parents' phone number by any chance?" Repeated almost nightly, that non-existent number dominated our conversations until Mom's death.

My annoyance with that pattern was real, but my frustration was obviously the least of the worrisome consequences of Mom's illness. At the suggestion of the folks at Boulder County Aging Services Division, I worked toward meeting Mom's nutritional needs by arranging for her to receive "Meals on Wheels" three times a week. This helpful program delivered a hot lunch at nominal cost. It also assured a friendly visitor who did not intrude by coming into the house, but who checked in from the door to see that Mom was safe at home. But, as with the horse led to water…there was no guarantee she would actually eat what was brought. Soon I noticed that the aluminum trays, mostly filled with food, were piling up in Mom's refrigerator and trash can. "Don't you like what they bring?" I asked.

"Oh yes, it tastes very good. But it never gets here on time." I was confused. They promised to deliver between 11:30 and noon, which is something of a spread when one is waiting to eat, I admit, but it didn't seem that long—to me. For someone with memory loss, however, five minutes might as well be a lifetime. My call to Mom around 11:15 on Wednesday to remind her that her nice lunch should be delivered *soon* didn't help.

"Oh really," would be her astonished response, "I didn't think they delivered on Sunday. I just ate my eggs."

Good Lord, the same eggs that have been in her refrigerator for months, I agonized? Friday, I called a little earlier to preempt the cooking. "Hi Mom, are you hungry yet? Your lunch will be delivered anytime now."

"I didn't know they'd come *today*," Mom's intonation conveyed her genuine surprise. "Thank you for letting me know. I think I'll wait for them outside so they don't have to come all the way to my door."

Glad for her interest in moving a bit again, I encouraged the idea. What could go wrong with Mom stretching her legs a little in a neighborhood she had called home for forty years?

WE HAD BEEN on this trek long enough that I should probably have foreseen trouble with Mom's excursions out to welcome her lunch. While I had hoped she might be regaining the tiniest measure of her self-sufficiency, quite the opposite was the case. Mom's desire, *need* really, to get out of her house signaled the beginning of what would soon force upon us the most painful, permanent dependency with which Mom would yet be shackled. Mom's inability to sort and order her world had turned restless and she started wandering. Initially, Mom would meet the "Meals on Wheels" delivery car in her driveway. When they arrived a little late, or Mom left her house too early, impatience drove her to walk farther up the block. Occasionally, before I left Mom's house for home, a neighbor would stop me to confide that she'd seen Mom heading up the street. Did I know that, and was it alright? The answer was no on both counts, but I felt powerless to stop it. I couldn't *make* Mom stay home, could I?

Boulder does have good resources for the elderly. So while everyone agreed that it was indeed impossible for me to keep Mom from striking out on whatever mission might come to her diseased mind, registering her with the police department's "ID for Me" program would assure easy identification if she got lost.

The young officer who applied the ID bracelet was kind and thoughtful throughout the process, and when all was said and done it did look relatively inoffensive on Mom's arm. But it did not escape her (or my) notice that Mom herself could not remove it. She still reluctantly agreed that it was probably best to wear the bracelet, "… just in case I fall or something." It was neither as lovely nor as benign as the many turquoise and silver armbands Dad used to buy for Mom when we first discovered the beauty of southwest American Indian jewelry. She always wore those proudly, and I thought being accustomed to their weight on her wrist might help her tolerate this new indignity. At least it helped me feel better as I found Mom venturing farther and farther from home. She was now frequently standing at the intersection a whole block from her house when I arrived for my visit. And although Mom's eyes brightened with recognition as I pulled my car over to her, I suspected that her meeting me there was entirely accidental. She would have been standing at that corner even if I hadn't arrived, waiting for who knows how long, for who knows what.

I had always thought my greatest anguish would come

from seeing Mom so physically disabled *some day* that, with her immobile, I would always know exactly where she was. After a lifetime of cheering her independent ideas and actions, I dreaded the notion of her unfailingly planted on her couch for hours without company, diversion, or stimulus. A phone call one late afternoon changed that vision. It was infinitely worse NOT to know where she was.

"Uhm, Mom, I don't want to worry you." Curtis's voice on my office phone was uncharacteristically tentative: "But do you know where Omi went? She wasn't here when I came home." Running on a tight daily schedule between teaching and coaching, Curtis needed to leave for the team practice in the late afternoon, but he wasn't comfortable doing so without knowing where Mom was.

Neither was I. "I'm on my way, Hon. Thanks!" My heart pounding in my throat, I gave my boss the news and with everyone urging me to "Go. Go," I raced out of the office. Oh dear Mom! It wasn't winter yet, but September evenings get cold fast once the sun goes down. And whether it was the icy grip of fear in my heart, or the brisk breeze coming across the Flatirons from the west, I was chilled to the core and felt myself warming only with the car's heater finally blowing hot air directly in my face. I left campus much too fast, considering the many students chattering on their phones and strolling aimlessly across the campus streets. "They're on their own in this; I can only take care of so many people at once," I illogically excused myself as I ripped south onto Broadway.

Racing onto Mom's street, I caught a glimpse of her wandering down the sidewalk from the bus stop about four blocks from her house. She was huddled into herself but unmistakable in a disheveled summer dress, exposed goose-pimpled skin, and windblown hair. I pulled over and left the car parked vaguely in the vicinity of the curb before running up to hold her. "Mom, what are you doing out here?"

Mom gratefully hugged me back but obviously didn't share my concern about her condition. "I waited for three buses so I could help my Mum carry the groceries. She's not very strong, you know. But she never came."

101

I whispered a short prayer to whomever is watching over the infirm for keeping Mom off the bus, then convinced her to get in the car and let me drive her home. But she continued to search intently up and down the street. "My Mum said she'd come visit today and I need to help her get here."

Expecting her Mum's visit was not a passing obsession for her. During repeated instances of retrieving Mom from somewhere on the street, I would remind myself to calm down. She *was* wearing that "ID for Me" bracelet. Even if she got on a bus without our knowledge some day, the driver could eventually discover her identity and get in touch with me. But what if she got off in an unfamiliar neighborhood? Or she might have, either accidentally or according to her misguided logic, boarded the bus to Denver. I had to be available by phone twenty-four hours a day; and from work to marriage, I was becoming an exceedingly poor participant in other parts of my life.

The strain of constant worry and sadness was beginning to show on Curtis too. What began three years earlier as a beneficial living arrangement for them both was turning into a nightmare. Mom had taken to wandering into his bedroom unannounced any time of the day or night. Although she ignored her own nutrition, she'd ask repeatedly whether she could get Curtis something to eat. He could say yes or no to her queries, but she'd be back two minutes later, or ten, with the same question. Although Curtis responded each time, Mom's forgetting meant that effectively she never received an answer; and Curtis had no privacy. While he needed more than ever to get away, a combination of love, guilt and frustration kept him stuck in place. Both he and Mom were trapped by Mom's disturbed mind and restless body ghosting through the house.

SOMETHING HAD TO change, but what were our options? When Mom and I could still talk coherently about growing older, Mom was adamant, like most of us, about wanting to stay at home. Try as I might, it was looking more and more like that was yet another in the litany of things I could not provide for her. Or more accurately, in addition to so much else I no longer understood about Mom's life, I didn't know where "home" was for her. And since she couldn't articulate that, I was powerless to help her feel "at home" even in her own house—the only place I knew to be her accessible home.

I also couldn't dissuade her from ambling along the street when I knew the person she was expecting would never walk from the bus to meet her. I had no way of helping her find herself in a time and space setting relevant to this world, because she could no longer recognize the clues I assumed would unfailingly remind her of who she was.

My impotence was made rudely clear around our afternoon cup-of-coffee ritual. Mom and I liked lots of milk in our cup and joked often about preferring "a little coffee in our milk." To make it just right, coffee and milk needed to produce the smooth sun-tanned brown of Colorado's late summer prairies. The right strength of fresh coffee mixed in with the right amount of milk yielded our perfect brew. At one point, however, when I asked Mom if her coffee *looked* right, she turned to me with a blank expression. In turn, my mind also went blank: *how* could she not know that, like me, she was a person who always wanted lots of milk in her coffee? I could no longer be the mirror reminding her that the face she was seeing in our togetherness was her own.

I could, in the end, *do* precious little—except, as people increasingly urged—try to keep her *safe*. Considering that on many levels Mom was still a mature adult, I wasn't so sure I agreed that her safety was my main goal.

"Really," Ute and I wondered out loud, "is keeping her *safe* sufficient justification for locking her up?" I've never believed that our notions of *saving* creatures from the natural hazards of the wild justify our condemning them to a cage. Wild animals, they say, are so safe in a "nice" zoo. If I thought a bird deserved freedom, could I disregard that principle with someone as important to me as my own mother? Of course I could, and I would. After all, how could I let her wander the streets, lonely, confused, and unaware of her precarious situation?

First, Ute and I considered at length whether Mom could move in with either of us. At least, we reasoned, she'd be in a familiar setting with family. But would it really be helpful? Neither Ute nor I were in a position to quit our jobs. With or without live-in care during our daytime absence, Mom would have been even more isolated and alone in our homes than she currently felt living somewhere she'd lived for decades but no longer recognized as her own. And if the idea of having Mom living with us might have comforted us for a while, we did finally come to accept reality. The reason we were faced with this dilemma was because Mom didn't even know where she was in her own home. How did we imagine she'd recognize, let alone be at ease, in ours? Of course, she would never be so.

That left a very short list of possible solutions. Mom couldn't stay at home without constant help which, even if available, she would most likely reject. Living with either of us would be no help to her. We also agreed unequivocally that a nursing home would not be appropriate for Mom as long as she was so "high-functioning." As we thought about it, it was beginning to look suspiciously like we had no list at all! Mom, never knowing that we needed one, persisted with her observation that "everything is fine."

I, on the other hand, had to admit that at that time I'd never been further from fine. In order to keep things moving forward, Paul sought information about what we saw as our last hope—residential facilities in our area. The two of us also made another appointment with a Boulder County Resource Specialist to learn all we could about services available for Mom. When all was said and done we found the choices limited and the costs astronomical. Once the word-games we were playing could no longer conceal the fact that we were, essentially, talking about nursing home care, I dissolved in tears. The counselor stood up, embraced me, and said gently, "Chris, *you* aren't causing your Mom's pain. The disease is." Those kind words calmed me, and as Paul and I ate sandwiches along Mom's beloved Boulder Creek Path, we resolved to visit assisted living facilities for something acceptable.

By then we knew that it wouldn't be easy but we were

prepared to search long and hard for a place good enough for Mom. For reasons of appropriateness more than quality, our search was almost in vain. First, we visited an assisted living complex. The degree of assistance available there did vary with each resident's needs and we were pleasantly surprised at how homey the gardens, grounds, and commons areas felt. Each room was equipped with a stoveless kitchen, and the unit then available for occupancy had a huge west-facing window with a broad view of Boulder's foothills. It was also within a five-minute drive from our house and I could almost picture Mom there—until we stepped out of the room we'd looked at and I tried to remember at which end of the long corridor the elevator was located. Lost, I turned around once or twice in that hallway, identical to all the others, and it struck me like a thunderbolt. If Mom didn't know her way around the home she'd lived in for decades, she couldn't possibly find her way around an unfamiliar building. She'd never have found the dining room or anyplace else in that building. Mom was well beyond that level of "assistance."

Next we visited a home with a good reputation for its "progressive care" units offering both skilled nursing care and a secured Alzheimer's unit. Everything was sanitized and pleasant, but the long, high-ceilinged halls with rooms and open doors leading off them strongly suggested institutionalized living to us. So did the faces of the residents. We listened politely to the sales pitch. We even believed their printed statement of purpose, to provide a loving and reasonable solution for the elderly who could no longer live alone, and for their beleaguered families. But the moment we could politely do so we fled, knowing that this wasn't a solution for Mom either. I cried often that weekend.

My weariness must have shown when I arrived at the office Monday morning. Still, a courageous colleague who did not expect the usual "just fine" for an answer left me an opening: "How is your search for a place for your Mom going, Chris?"

I had myself in hand sufficiently to keep from dissolving again, or maybe I was just out of tears, but I could not contain my sense of utter helplessness. "Not great," seemed a vast understatement.

"You know," my friend continued, "I have a friend who is the nursing director at Mountainview in Denver. She thinks it's the best memory care facility around, and whenever I've visited there I've been very impressed. I hear they've opened a new facility just south of Boulder."

Those few words did not heal Mom's disease, put an end to my role as chief caregiver, or eliminate Curtis's sadness at watching his Omi disappear. But they did lead us to a "Memory Care Residence" that would make all those hard realities bearable.

Making Camp: Autumn 2003

*"I make quilts as fast as I can to keep my family warm, and as
beautiful as I can to keep my heart from breaking"*
–18th Century Pioneer Woman's Diary

THE FIRST TIME Paul and I entered Mountainview we realized that it was different from other places we'd visited. Mind
you, I was in no mood to be seduced; this whole process of trying
to find the right place for Mom had left me worn out and wary,
to say the least. But as Paul and I walked into the warm atmo-
sphere of Mountainview's community areas, we must have
looked like cartoon characters: depressed and befuddled in the
first frame; whirling wide-eyed faces toward each other in the
next; and in a third, a light bulb above our grinning faces in
the notion balloon. The hope born of *possibility* came to us at
the same instant!

Our lengthy interview with Debbie, the community relations director, was not in a sterile office removed from the life of
the facility, but in the commons area open to the life at Mountainview. At one point a resident walked into our meeting, sat
down and nonchalantly inserted comments into our conversation. Although none of us could understand her contribution,
Debbie greeted her warmly and thanked her for her input as
she headed off again into her own world. Two women holding
hands shuffled by more often than I could count, yet greeted us
as new faces each time they came by. Once we got up to tour
the building, a silent resident's hand slid tentatively into mine.
Used to holding a frail hand, I gently closed my fingers around
Carol's and she hung on while we walked together until a different destination led her elsewhere while we continued on to

visit *Santa Fe House*. Carol, we learned, had been an enthusiastic and dedicated hiker.

Mountainview contains four separate "houses" built at the corners of the community areas. Each "house" has a name, 13 private residence rooms, a sitting area with plants, TV, stereo, and bulletin board, and its own kitchen area with dining room. Before entering by the front door, one crosses an attractive porch with flowers along the wooden railing and chairs to sit in while watching the world go by. The whole place is carpeted and nothing—not the Wellness Office, or the large walking gardens outside, the intimate dining areas in each house, or the library and beauty salon—nothing suggests that this is an institution.

There is not a single long, dead-end corridor to be found at Mountainview. Whenever one leaves a "house" and starts walking around to join a group in the commons areas, or to search for a friend (or a *new* acquaintance who has also lived there for years) in another "house," one invariably ends up exactly where one started. This is an essential feature for folks compelled by some force within them to move forward without ever knowing where they started, where they're headed, and least of all why they're on that particular errand. Unlike the assisted living facility we had visited the week before, I couldn't have gotten confused here even if Mountainview had had an elevator to be found!

Something about the lay-out of that place is utterly sensible and comfortable. It is thoughtfully designed for adults with, yes, a terrible disease, but with no less humanity, dignity, and worth for their affliction. As we entered *Santa Fe House,* a dog and cat ran over to greet us, but quickly found each other's company more entertaining than ours and rolled blissfully entangled around the living room. "Mom would be surrounded by animals here," I thought happily to myself as we were shown into the room that was then available. I noticed the large crabapple tree just outside the window and imagined its bright, pink spring blossoms as well as Mom's bed, chair, TV, dressing mirror, and important pictures and wall hangings in that setting. It occurred to me that Mountainview just might work!

We scheduled a residency evaluation for Mom, and rather than "escaping," as we had from the other facilities, we walked out energized. Paul, with his arm over my shoulder, summarized it well. "I saw more Life in our first two minutes there than in the hours at the other places." He was so right.

Now don't let my enthusiasm fool you. Mountainview was nice, to be sure, but no one living there was truly at *Home*. With none of the welcoming features of an entrance, from the inside, the front door was disguised to blend into the wall and escape the residents' notice. A small code box beside it marked the passage into that other world accessible only to those who could remember the correct number sequence to "Open Sesame." Rather than discreetly stashed in pocket or purse, the private room key dangled visibly from each resident's wrist on coiled, brightly colored plastic bands. That didn't assure that someone with dementia would be able to find his or her room without assistance, or recognize it as their own when they got there. But having a key to one's private place lent a sense of dignity and autonomy to persons losing both at a very rapid pace.

Table conversations were not as you and I would remember them from Sunday dinners. Beyond the inarticulate yes's and no's coming from murky memory, with an occasional complaint that a tablemate had something on her plate that the offended one couldn't find on his until it was pointed out to him, mealtime was a mostly silent, mechanical operation. Dessert, though, reliably brought pleasure to the routine. You might come across a resident inappropriately dressed. Or not dressed at all. And you might notice chairs, seasonal decorations, and accent pillows constantly rearranged by that cruel game the forgetting mind plays of endlessly challenging its owner to remember why these items are so placed and what the heck their purpose is.

In the end, though, this isn't "Home," because no one ever *wants* to live here. Mom wouldn't have either if she had understood what we were up to! Oh, sure, as all responsible adults must at some point, Mom and I too had talked about the *future*. "Some day," we agreed, yard work and household chores would prove too much for her, even with Curtis's or hired help. Already at that time Mom was hinting that she no longer felt particularly safe in the house alone, especially at night. And when the future seemed sufficiently far enough away to safely address it, Mom and I even paid a deposit at an apartment complex for seniors in downtown Boulder. Mom was placed on their five-year waiting list. When we received notice that Mom was eligible for space sometime in 1999, I remember sending it back gratefully indicating that Mom "wasn't ready" for such downsizing. They moved her name back to the bottom of the list. As I thought about it, we should have heard from them around the time we were looking at Mountainview. She wouldn't have been ready then, either.

Now that the future had undeniably caught up with us, there was little left to explain to Mom, and less for her to comprehend. I'd mention at every opportunity how much we worried about Mom in her house alone. What if she should fall, or get confused while she's out and about? Who would be there to help her? I started trying to prepare her for the changes we were planning for her with broad hints: "You know Mom, if we could find a private place for you, close to us, we would all feel so much better if you didn't have to worry about fixing meals or cleaning house." I ignored my conscience nagging unhelpfully that I might mention we'd already found that place, and instead continued, "Don't you sometimes feel pretty isolated here now that Jean no longer drives? And since Greta had to move to Denver you don't get to see your friends very often anymore anyway."

Mom's own assessment of her life, and I suspect her genuinely held perception, remained uncharacteristically illusionary. After almost two years of not participating in her political discussion group, she insisted, "Well I only missed my group a couple of times; *this* week I can take the bus downtown and go back." She never did do so, of course.

Mom's early November intake interview for residency at Mountainview revealed that she was definitely an appropriate candidate. Another exam by her physician confirmed that assessment and sealed our decision without Mom ever comprehending what all of that was about. I, however, understood all too well that I needed to make plans—because that's what I do in a crisis and because there was no "good" time to do the difficult thing we were arranging for Mom. Quite certain that her illness would not improve, and fairly sure that there were no better alternatives, I started writing down-payment checks and filling out piles of paperwork. Move-in was scheduled for Saturday, November 29, 2003.

I thought a Saturday preferable since that was when Mom normally went to the hairdresser. I could drop her off knowing she would be safe there for a couple of hours while Paul, Curtis and I worked at Mom's house. We'd throw the essential and familiar things I wanted Mom to have in her new place into a truck Curtis had borrowed. Then I'd pick Mom up from the beauty shop and take her out to lunch, assured that my two guys were scrambling to get everything moved into her room on the other end. By early afternoon, in time for her daily rest, I'd bring Mom to her *bed* at Mountainview, and hope I could still face myself when it was all over. I couldn't imagine how on earth I'd actually walk away leaving Mom behind for the first time, but I clung to the hope that what everyone was saying would actually prove to be the case. "This will be much rougher for you, Chris, than for your Mom."

That assurance sounded good, but I wasn't betting on it. Being kidnapped from her own home and moved into an unfamiliar setting, with no say in the decisions or outcome, would have to be about as bad as it gets, wouldn't it? Guilt-ridden with my sense of betrayal, I wallowed in a monumental dose of self-pity about our doing the worst of all things to Mom. Even my previously unshakable ability to sleep failed me. I spent November nights tossing and turning. Though I had no stomach for Thanksgiving festivities, Paul faithfully cooked the traditional turkey dinner for the four of us. With physical effort, and emotional pretense, we choked down the meal.

To get us through the afternoon, we watched yet again the family video I had given Mom for Christmas long ago. For years Mom had loved viewing this record of happy family times in Germany, our early years in Boulder, and the arrival of Mom's

111

grandchildren. That day Mom was even more appreciative of the video than before, maybe because it was all new to her. Amazed but overjoyed with such a testimony of our family's life, Mom was certain that she had "never seen that nice film before!" This indication that we were, after all, planning the right thing for Mom provided me a bit of reassurance, but no comfort.

The following day, Paul and I went to Mountainview to prepare Mom's room. We made sure that the phone was connected. Armed with coat racks and curtain rods, bathroom supplies and picture hooks, we stored, hung, nailed and placed whatever we could pre-arrange. Paul listened patiently as I, for the hundredth time, talked him through my detailed sketch showing what should go where. We practiced the door code on the key-pad and confirmed that staff would help with access and unloading when Paul and Curtis arrived the next day. Finally, we confirmed that Debbie would be the manager on duty to assist with introductions and to help Mom settle in. With the vain hope that if I said it enough I might actually convince myself, an inner voice repeated my mantra: "Mom has a private room with a bath! She remains close to us. And we can continue to see each other for our afternoon coffee or whatever else we want to do together. Given Mom's health and where we've been so far, things won't really be *that* different..."

I knew, of course, that in fact everything was about to change drastically for Mom. And if on some level I also knew that the disease was at fault rather than me, there was no doubt that in this specific instance I was the agent of everything looming before us. Saturday's sun rose much too late for my mind, which was impatient to get this over with, but far too early for undertaking the deed at all. Feeling my anxiety more intensely than an overseer's whip, Paul and Curtis worked like men possessed. They took seriously my uncertainty about how long I could keep Mom from wanting to go home once she was finished at the hairdresser. They labored under my consequent near-panic-level insistence that her room simply *must* be ready, and recognizably hers—whenever we showed up. I left them a tall order. But if I've always loved and appreciated those two dear men in my life, when Mom and I arrived to behold what would from then on be her world, I wanted to weep with gratitude for their accomplishment.

Perhaps somewhat puzzled by it all, Mom obviously didn't share our sense of apprehension at what was happening. She was even mildly interested throughout her introduction to Mountainview. In fact, rather than being upset, by the time we ushered her into her room and encouraged her to sit on her bed and survey the new surroundings, she relaxed with recognition. "Oh, yes, there is my painting of Lübeck. And look, the pictures of my Mum and Dad are on that wall!"

Even as the designer of our tightly-orchestrated plan, it took me a while to realize that Paul and Curtis had actually pulled it off! With Mom's furniture, clothing, lamps, nick-knacks and mementos surrounding her, she looked, and seemed to feel, comfortably in place.

As we explained to Mom why this would be her place for a while and how all her things were here to make her comfortable, we used the language Ute wisely suggested by referring to Mountainview as a sanitarium. It was neither hospital nor nursing home, and her having to go someplace special to heal and recuperate, a "sanitarium" as we would refer to it in our native German, would make sense to Mom. She accepted this "sanitarium" so well that, on her good days, Mom continued to treat having a private room with her own key, an emergency call button, and meals prepared in an intimate dining room as something of a luxury. It seemed to her more like a hotel than the prison sentence to which I felt I was condemning her. As we left Mom in her new "home" I assured her I'd call her later to say good night, and would pick her up for church the next morning—as always. She readily agreed that things were just fine. All in all, it hadn't been *that* bad a start.

IT COULD HAVE been Mom's illness and her relentless forgetting that eased her transition to life at Mountainview. I think at least as influential was her ever-obliging, reasonable nature. Either way, the friends who tried to ease my sense of betrayal over the maneuver of abducting Mom from her house and committing her to Mountainview turned out to be mostly right. With a darned smooth start, it didn't get much worse over the coming months. At least not, that is, if we could cope with the fact that within days of settling into her room, Mom started planning, packing, and worrying over "going home." She ended most of our nightly "sleep tight" calls with the assertive and hopeful, "...and tomorrow I'm going home." When visiting friends promised to return soon, she'd firmly correct them. "Oh, but I won't be *here* anymore; I'll be home by then." And when I brought personal supplies or flowers, her initial pleasure quickly turned to annoyance. "I just don't know how to get all that stuff home tomorrow."

I've wished for few things as fervently as I've wanted to understand what Mom meant by "home." But when we left church after Mom's move to Mountainview and drove through the very neighborhood Mom called home for four decades, I breathed a sigh of relief each time it became clear again that *that* was not the area Mom longed to return to. As we waited at the intersection she must have crossed thousands of times, she looked at the street names and thoughtfully repeated, "Table Mesa Drive and Broadway. I should know where that is."

But she didn't. And while I despised what appeared to me Mom's horrible "lostness" from any place familiar to her, I also breathed a little easier. The weight of my guilt was lightened with each reminder that it was not the move to Mountainview that removed Mom from her "home." It was likely Mom's continuous questioning of the future that made her life at Mountainview bearable, and my conscience for having moved her there, more clear. And while her constant assertions about going home could be astonishing and occasionally exasperating, as long as Mom's statements were, to her mind, new with each telling, I was assured that her repetitions of them had not grown into the festering wounds that develop in those who can remember each dream repeatedly denied.

Take dinner, for example. It startled me each time Mom declared that she had to get home to fix some food. After all, she reasoned, "I've never eaten *here* before."

I didn't fight it anymore. "Oh, but the good thing about being here is you don't have to cook at all. They just let you know when the food is ready to eat," rolled easily off my tongue because I loved watching Mom's obvious relief when I reminded her that her meal was ready for her, fully prepared. For me it was ceaseless repetition, but for Mom (and that's all that mattered), that revelation was a pleasant surprise bringing relief again. And again.

With such relentless, sometimes jarring, evidence of Mom's decline, I was gradually coming to accept that by assuring her compassionate care and safety, we had done the best we could for Mom. I never stopped feeling that that could not fulfill my hopes for her, but with time I came to understand that my greatest fear would also not be realized: Mom's move into a professional care residence did not displace me as her main caregiver! On the contrary, I had to retain the role precisely *because* she was living in a medical facility. It has been shown repeatedly that residents in even the best institutions receive more informed and personalized attention when the family can intentionally participate in their care. It's the same principle, I suppose, that explains why children with parents actively involved in their education usually learn better.

I didn't care one whit about social or pedagogical theories suggesting what one ought or ought not to do, though. I'd made a promise to Mom (and myself) that after all our trips together she would not travel her final journey by herself. I was going to keep that promise. So I visited Mom daily. I didn't stop at the French bakery for "some nice pieces" anymore, but continued to bring fruit or cookies as an afternoon treat with the decaf I now fixed in the *Santa Fe House* kitchen. I joined in the singing, reading, and craft sessions, and using the same words consistently for clarity, I spent a good part of every day explaining to Mom where she was and why she was there. I shuttled her to our house for videos in the afternoon or lunch after church; and Paul, Curtis, and I attended every special event nicely pulled together by the Mountainview staff.

There was the first Christmas party we attended. We

could hear the music already underway long before we reached its source. Suddenly I began to worry that, as a professional musician with a lifelong knowledge of what "good" music should sound like, Mom would be mortified at joining in the off-beat, off-tune, just plain off voices coming from the social room. But, suddenly, as we were approaching them, Mom's face relaxed while her hand in mine calmly, happily, and correctly started to pick up the beat and bounce to the rhythm of "Jingle Bells." Her body and soul fully engaged with the tune, Mom did turn to me admitting that she didn't "know all the words." I had to chuckle as I reassured her, "Heck, none of us knows all the words, dear Mom." But here we were, singing anyway...together!

Candy canes from Santa gave way to a Valentine's Day dance and an Easter Brunch. The Mother's Day Tea was shortly followed by a Father's Day BBQ and somehow we'd made it into our first spring at Mountainview. Then Mom and I could enjoy walking and sitting in the lovely garden area surrounded by flowers, birds, and rabbits.

I spent so much time with Mom I wondered that the director didn't begin to charge me rent too! I knew it wasn't always easy for the staff to have me around, but I tried not to hover; and there were times when I could even be helpful with other residents. Above all, I set out to nurture my relationships with the staff. Employee turnover is a common problem in care facilities, and with every familiar and new face among them I found myself complimenting, cajoling, and critiquing everyone to assure that Mom's needs were, at least, understood. Better yet, of course, I pushed to have them met.

During that summer, Ute offered the same arrangements to be in Colorado for her time with Mom. Again she and her big, lovable dog, Winston, drove a third of the way across the continent to be here. And although boisterous and lively with his able-bodied family, Winston was exceedingly gentle when he visited Mom and other frail residents at Mountainview. I headed to Maine with a decidedly lighter heart, and Curtis had gotten into the habit of having dinner with his Omi at least once a week. I hoped Mom's family weren't making utter nuisances of ourselves. But by the time Mom had lived at Mountainview for six months, it had to be obvious to everyone there that we would continue to be ever present in Mom's life and available through all eventualities. At least that's how it appeared to us.

Unsettled Territory: Autumn 2004

"Great opportunities to help others seldom come,
but small ones surround us daily"
–Sally Koch

To SUSTAIN MY mental and physical strength on this trek with Mom, I had signed up for another half-marathon training program. The goal race was scheduled for early October in Monterey. As the time for travel planning approached, Paul offered to stay in Boulder to "take care of things," while Ute and I would have a sister-weekend on the California coast. Great idea! With Paul and Curtis at home, I could skip visiting Mom for three days. Though I didn't want to overplay this departure for such a short trip, I did catch myself holding Mom a bit tighter than usual before I left her room that Thursday evening. I assured Mom I'd call her the next day, "just like always," and after explaining my plans, left my full itinerary with the director at Mountainview. In large type it contained dates and details with my cell-phone number and that of the hotel where Ute and I would be staying. It further reminded staff that both Paul and Curtis would be close by and could be reached anytime at our home numbers. You have them on record, I added hopefully in a note at the bottom, but they're "listed again here on the sheet."

I was excited about getting away and running thirteen miles with friends along the ocean, but I especially looked forward to having time with Ute. We connected easily at the San Francisco airport at mid-day on a beautiful early-autumn

119

Friday. We chatted non-stop on the drive south in our rental car, and kept talking over a leisurely margarita followed by crab chowder so deliciously thick that a cup was a meal in itself. We strolled along the Monterey Marina, a mirror for the setting sun, before dropping content and tired onto our beds. "How nice," we agreed, as we rarely did as kids, "that we can place this *good night* call to Mom together."

The first time we dialed Mom's number, it was just after six in Colorado and we weren't surprised that no one answered. Mom was probably out and about. Besides, Ute and I still had plenty to catch up on. When next we tried it was close to 7:00 Mountain Time, Mom's bedtime. Ute and I exchanged puzzled glances as the phone rang and rang. Maybe they were showing a late movie at Mountainview and Mom had decided to watch it? It wasn't like her, but we didn't want to be alarmists. Several pieces of chocolate and half an hour later we tried again with still no answer. By now it was approaching 8:00 at Mom's place, and she was at least an hour late for her date with her beloved bed. Something wasn't right.

I called again, this time the main Mountainview number. It took a while before someone answered, and even longer before we were connected to the caregivers in *Santa Fe House*. Close to the edge now, Ute and I were wondering out loud, "What the hell is going on?" before finally someone in charge of Mom's care came on the line. I explained that we'd been trying to reach Mom for two hours, couldn't get her, and could they, please, tell us where she is?

A short, hollow silence was followed by the clipped words of a young, confused voice on the other end, "Oh, uhm, Ilse is at the hospital."

"She is what... ?" My composure was shot. "They took Mom to the hospital," I updated Ute as her face registered the bewilderment that overtakes us when we've learned just enough to know something is wrong, but not what or why. "What do you mean? What happened?" Our questions spilled forth in rapid-fire succession. "Which hospital? Is she okay?" Obviously she wasn't and the realization made me furious. "Why," I was shouting now, "weren't we contacted?" And before the befuddled voice on the other end of the line could respond, we confronted her with the most troubling question to rise out of our distress. "WHO is with her?" The hesitant voice, which I later learned belonged to Vickie, Mom's caregiver that night, stammered while Ute and I made it clear that we did not want to hear what she was about to say. "Do not," I said, as if a sufficiently emphatic tone could change the past, "*do not* tell us she's going through this alone!"

Bit by ill-fated bit the story unfolded. Mom had fallen trying to get up from the dinner table. She had hit the back of her head on the floor and could not get up, either by herself or with help. Emergency services were summoned, and the attendants rolled Mom to the ambulance. They would stay with her until they reached the hospital emergency room. Strictly speaking, she was never alone.

But that did little for our vision of Mom having to go through that experience without the support of someone familiar by her side. For years Mom and I had walked through crises hanging on to each other, and I wanted someone to be holding her hand now! Besides, Ute and I had worked ourselves into angry incredulity by now. It was not just a matter of support; what about legal representation of Mom's medical choices? Wasn't she at Mountainview precisely because she couldn't speak coherently for herself anymore? Who, at that hospital, knew that she had a notarized DNR[12] on file? And not to belabor the point, but *why* was no one from the family contacted?

Apparently, I would later learn, Vickie had tried to reach me. Unfortunately, all three copies of the carefully crafted schedule of my trip, with my whereabouts and all the contact information for Mom's extended family, were locked safely in the director's office. So instead of calling my cell phone, or our hotel room in Monterey, the caregiver, using the standard reference book, tried to reach me at home. Without revealing her

---

12   Mom had long ago legally signed the "do not resuscitate" order then on file at Mountainview. The document does not prevent palliative care, but makes legally binding an individual's wish not to be "brought back to life" via heroic measures should s/he be in sufficient distress to be found without breath or pulse.

identity or reason for calling, Vickie had simply asked to speak to Chris. When Paul told her I was not available, but invited her to leave a message, she thanked him politely and hung up. Rather than trying anyone else on the long list of emergency references we had on record at Mountainview, Vickie's next panicked call was for an ambulance. From then on, Mom was on her own.

Our first call to Paul would change that. Dismayed that the person who had asked for me on the phone earlier had not given such important information, he wasted no time getting to the hospital to be the first familiar face in Mom's chaotic evening. Our next call reached the emergency room nurse and doctor to whom Mom had been assigned. We assured everyone that my husband was on his way. He'd be there within minutes to help calm Mom and sort things out.

At last we got to talk to Mom directly, and although she sounded drained from her experience, she didn't seem too distressed. She had no memory of falling and no understanding of where she was after the fall. She did, however, express tremendous relief at not being "down there" on the floor anymore. With no recollection of how she landed there, her only thoughts were of getting off the ground as quickly as possible. She couldn't manage it though, and lying next to her chair gave her enough time to realize that, as she said again and again, "I didn't know how to get back up." When these "nice men" arrived to help her off the floor she was simply grateful. I don't know what else she knew or feared. She was, however, very glad to see Paul and went to sleep in her hospital room assured by his promise to return first thing the next morning.

Ute and I talked late into the night. Mostly we tried to sort out what seemed to us to have been Mountainview's phenomenal failure of communication, internal and external. How could they not have known that they needed to contact us at the time of Mom's accident? By the time we finally settled into silence, there were only a few hours left for sleep. Even those brought little rest. We started calling Boulder again as early the next morning as was reasonable. When we reached the hospital personnel we were informed that Mom's x-rays revealed she was suffering from a light case of pneumonia. No doubt that's why she had felt so weak and had fallen. But after some fluids and antibiotics, the doctor assured us, Mom would be ready to go "home" later that day. Mom's nurse further explained that the doctor had ordered several additional tests, just to confirm that Mom really was as sound as she appeared. "Your Mom," she wanted us to know, "really is coping very well."

Overall, the hospital staff made only one observation about Mom's condition they thought noteworthy. "Ilse seems to be a little confused," the nurse explained somewhat apologetically. "Somehow she's got it into her head that her son-in-law is coming."

I was going to suggest that it might have been significant to note that Mom was suffering from severe dementia and memory loss, but I just shook my head in disbelief. Apparently that medical facility had no knowledge of who that person, my Mom, was and what had contributed to her being there. Although Mom's accident had occurred at a secure, residential memory-care facility, which was listed as her permanent home, in the past twenty-four hours (with the attendance of the staff at a professional memory care facility and the diagnosis of a registered nurse included!), the only person who knew what was going to happen that morning was Mom! Paul was beside her by eight the next morning and when Mom was finally released, he drove her to Mountainview to see her settled comfortably back in her own bed.

In California, it was cold and raining steadily when I got up at five-thirty the next morning to run a disappointing race. I don't recommend running thirteen miles after spending two nights hanging over the toilet purging yourself of anger and worry. After my slowest half-marathon ever, I was glad to drag myself to the finish line, and even happier to have Ute there to wrap her warm winter coat around me. I barely made it to the first row of port-a-potties before upchucking what I didn't have in my stomach; and as soon as we'd gingerly made our way back to the hotel, I threw up again. But Ute got me my cure-all, sparkling seltzer water, and fed me bland sweet crackers that stayed down. Some rest and a shower revived me for our drive back to the airport. When we separated to head for our respective departure gates, we agreed how good it had been to handle this hard time together. As we parted, Ute held me and said earnestly, "You know, I don't think we should let this stuff make us sick."

She was right, and in my subsequent efforts to leave behind my belief that I could control Mom's disease, her advice was invaluable. At the time, though, the best medicine was the fact that I was on my way home!

Mountainview's executive director contacted me Monday morning to assume full responsibility for how the accident had been mishandled by her staff. She offered repeated apologies and partial explanations. Stringent Health Insurance Portability and Accountability Act (HIPPA) regulations make healthcare providers hesitant to divulge private patient information, especially over the telephone. But Julie made no excuses. Mountainview's policy unquestionably required that, in an emergency, family of residents always be contacted first. Even with the details of my absence not available to her, Mom's caregiver should have known to introduce herself fully to Paul, explain that there had been an accident, and made a greater effort to locate or get a message to me. Vickie should have followed protocol.

Julie also filed an official "incident report" before we met with all involved staff to discuss just what had gone wrong and how to prevent such a breakdown of communication in the future. Finally, we scheduled another care conference during which we spelled out all of Mom's care needs and contact information once again. Ute participated in these conferences by long-distance and speakerphone, and Curtis and Paul stood by me during the "in person" meetings. We were united in our indignation: carting Mom off to the hospital alone, with her uninformed family minutes away, was unacceptable to us. Pure and simple, there was nothing else to say about that. But moving Mom to another facility was out of the question because we were well aware that, for all our talk, there was really nowhere else for her. So we were very grateful for Mountainview's receptive approach to addressing the weekend's disaster. What would we have done without it?

But I, too, had another lesson to learn. A year earlier I'd faced the fact that I could no longer assure Mom's safety in every situation. But the realization that I couldn't expect Mountainview to do so either proved even tougher to swallow. It dawned on me that I'd best get good and used to the fact that no one could. If serious errors in Mom's protection and care could be avoided, it was hard to realize nevertheless that the progression of Mom's disease would likely bring a constant change in her and her needs. The moment I insisted that something in her routine must be handled *just so*, her condition would change just enough to make that particular approach no longer feasible.

Mom used to love open windows. Like any good German, she was raised to believe that "fresh air" is not only refreshing but also therapeutic. She would allow at least a moment's worth of outside air to blow the cobwebs out of the house regardless of how cold or wet the weather. Consequently, I had gone to great lengths to "train" the *Santa Fe House* staff to open the windows Mom could no longer manage herself daily, even if only a crack. I assured them Mom really needed fresh air!

The nurses and caregivers had become so diligent in opening Mom's window that I was angry the first time I arrived to find her room hot and stuffy with the windows tightly shut. Instead of with a civil hello, I greeted Mom harshly. "Why didn't someone open your windows?"

It was not the welcome I wanted to share with Mom, and regretted my over-reaction even more when she calmly replied, "Oh they wanted to, but I told them it's much too cold today."

I had forgotten that Mom was not the same person I had known my whole life. In some ways, she wasn't the same person I had visited yesterday. Possibly, at that very minute, she wasn't even the woman the caregiver had met that morning—the one who at *that* time did not want her window opened. I struggled to accept that someone else was beginning to know some of Mom as well as I had known her. On the other hand, it was reassuring to realize that, if I would allow it, I could build a compassionate partnership with the Mountainview staff. All of our heads would be better than mine alone at discovering how best to meet Mom's needs in this unpredictable state of her mind.

When I visited Mom upon my return from California, she was glad to see me, but not especially so. She didn't remember going to the hospital and even at the time apparently didn't grasp what made the rest of us so upset: that she had done so alone. Mom did mention her anxiety at finding herself, inexplicably, on the floor and not knowing how to get up. But it wasn't long until some "nice men" helped her, and whatever happened afterwards was lost to Mom.

Just as well, I thought gratefully before I noticed the shadow on Mom's face that indicated she was already on another topic. Finally she gave voice to that quizzical look in her eyes that indicated something was troubling her. "How did you find me *here?*" I was sitting on her bed stroking her hand as she continued, "I've never been to this place before. It's lucky you found me."

I held her hand more firmly, "Yup, I'm really glad I found you!" Here is where I shook my finger at her in the mock gesture of a teacher making an important point. "Just remember," I grinned at her broadly, "you can't get away from me. I'll always find you!"

I came to use this promise regularly to assure Mom that, whether she knew or not, I would always know where she was. In response, the disbelief on Mom's face instantly turned playful. A huge smile brightened her face and while absent-mindedly patting my hand she said happily, "That's nice. That's what my Mum always tells me too."

Longing for Home:
2004-2005

"Tell me not in mournful number
Life is but an empty dream!
For the soul is dead that slumbers
And things are not what they seem
Life is real. Life is earnest!
And the grave is not its goal;
Dust thou art. To dust returnest
Was not spoken of the soul"
–Henry Wadsworth Longfellow

IT WAS COMFORTING to realize that I could do far worse than be my grandmother in Mom's eyes. As I thought of it, I *did* do worse every time I brought my outdated notions of who Mom was into her room with me. Admittedly, Mom's life was far from anything I would have wished for her, but it was nevertheless *her* life. If I wasn't going to spoil the few remaining pleasures Mom and I had left to share, I'd best figure out how to give up my frantic clinging to control. No matter where Mom thought she was, or who she saw me as, after I returned from cold, wet northern California I realized that my promise that I would "always find her" would require my ability to recognize *her*. Rather than trying to resurrect the woman who was my mother for decades, I vowed to be more ready to appreciate who she was at that moment.

I felt released enough by that new commitment to notice that the leaves outside were starting to turn. The wind was echoing the weather predictions (or is it the other way around?) of early snows. It was definitely fall. And with its breezes came

127

my realization that just maybe this year I'd get to reclaim my favorite season. Might this autumn at last be the one to again tame the extremes of the other three seasons? Rather than my making trips to Mountainview every single day, Paul and I resumed our long-neglected habit of spending Fridays in the mountains. Later Paul would fix us snacks and margaritas, and I began the weekend by celebrating that I was a wife as well as a daughter.

It wasn't easy, but occasionally I even drove straight home after work and began limiting my trips to Mountainview to four or five times a week. That forced me to allow others to care for Mom. And whether visiting Mom, training for my next race, or going on short trips with Paul, I took Ute's words to heart. Mom's illness never again made me sick to my stomach.

Mom's slow, noticeable decline did, however, continue. And I tried to adapt to that. I was determined to stop finishing Mom's sentences for her. Especially since I knew the exact words Mom would utter next, waiting for her to actually do so could be excruciating; but I learned to curb my impatience. Our conversations cycled through the same exchange. With every repetition of Mom's intention to go "home," I recited my litany for why it was good for her to stay there. "Until you get stronger, it's really better for you not to live alone. Here the caregivers can always help."

In turn, Mom answered like a petulant child. "My Mum's at home. She can take care of me."

No matter how many times we spoke those words, I always wished I could have seen into Mom's mind and learned whether the "home" she imagined was Dassendorf, or Buller-deich, or some other place of her childhood. "Well, right." That first part of my response a blatant lie, I did then find my way back to the gospel truth with, "But we so love having you close to us, dear Mom."

Mom conceded, "Yes, that *is* nice." Her acquiescence granted me a short reprieve from the guilt that lingered from the "kidnapping" regardless of how often I reminded myself that whatever "home" Mom was referring to, it was not her house in South Boulder from which we had moved her to Mountainview.

It occurred to us, too, that Mom's sense of home may not have been in this world at all. Ute and I have wondered whether Mom might actually have been longing to die when she talked of "going home." The image consoled us. With the Christian concept of heaven it's even conceivable to think of Mom finding her parents there. But somehow I didn't believe the home she longed for was an other-worldly one. Given Mom's fierce reliance on practical, hard and fast cues for sorting out her thoughts, I didn't think she had the mental acuity any longer to conceive of such an esoteric peace. In the end, it probably didn't matter what Mom longed for or where she considered home to be. It was not a place to which we could take her. All my good will and effort notwithstanding, the sadness at my inability to soothe her yearning was only slightly less painful than the shame I still felt at having moved her from her house. So I settled for helping her feel that she was in the right place *there.*

With November on the horizon, a dear friend called to say she thought it was her turn to host a birthday party. Never one to turn down a celebration, especially one thrown in my honor, I thought it a great idea. But I didn't want anything to remind Mom that it was my birthday! I could just picture her anguish. "What about presents and the Bienenstich?" she'd fret. Who, after all, would cook Chris's tomato soup just the way she liked it? Jennifer understood, and we agreed on getting our families together in just that spirit, without flowers, cards, or birthday acknowledgment of any kind.

As soon as I picked Mom up for "brunch at Jen's," I realized that we needn't have worried. Although Jen had been a family friend for decades, Mom had no idea where we were going. "Where does Jen live?" and "Why are we going there?" revealed her total lack of awareness.

It was good to be together, and without a hint of awkwardness, we toasted each other, and Life, and the privilege of family and friends at a "non-birthday" get-together. Mom, however, got little pleasure from being in an unfamiliar place with people she really didn't know. I brought her back to Mountainview confused and exhausted and she was happy to get into her bed to "rest up." Although I had been surrounded by love and laughter, I too fell into bed as soon as Paul and I got home. I like to think that my need to cry at that point was brought on by that harsh reminder of all Mom had lost. Had she really just attended a party, the sun chilly and low on the Halloween witches and hay bales still decorating the neighborhood, without an inkling that it was her daughter's birthday? But the tears didn't come easily. Instead of washing away my grief, they choked me and burned in my chest, bubbling like magma escaping the earth. No altruistic compassion, this, but a peevish, bitter flow I couldn't have controlled if I'd wanted to. And I didn't want to! All the medical diagnoses and rational explanations refused to bring comfort, when at the end of that day all that remained with me was that I had been forgotten. By my Mom!

The one-year anniversary of Mom's move to Mountainview passed unnoticed. The Thanksgiving decorations were quickly replaced by the traditional red and green Christmas garlands. Along the way Mom's demeanor grew quieter. She spent hours in her bed resting all day and could still sleep soundly at night. Her sense of "getting better" took on new meaning as she would frequently say that she'd like to just stay comfortable, there in her bed. The only problem for her was that she couldn't reach her parents. "I need to let my Mum know that I'm staying here today. I've been in school all day and that was very good for me."

Mom had started referring to the various music and craft activities at Mountainview as her classes and lectures. And since she obviously got some pleasure from them (or from their availability even if she didn't attend them), I assured her that her parents would want her to enjoy those sessions and remain in a safe, comfortable place. She perked up instantly. "Did you talk with my Mum?"

"Well, you know they don't have a phone in Dassendorf. But I did get them a message. They know you are fine here." Often this explanation was sufficient for Mom and her relief would be palpable.

When it wasn't, Mom took to writing letters to her parents. Tucked in a neat airmail envelope would be several pages of carefully hand-written thoughts expressing how much Mom missed her Mum and Dad at her beloved childhood home in northern Germany. She always closed with a notation that

she understood why her parents, being busy and without a phone, couldn't easily get in touch with her. But she nevertheless pleaded with them to try.

It was heartbreaking enough for me to take these letters from Mom's room with the promise to "mail" them, when the notion that they might reach her parents still comforted her. But on this journey no solution lasted forever and no remedy remained foolproof. Before long, the reassurance written communication brought was also taken from Mom. Initially she could no longer conceptualize what it would take to reach her distant parents. That was soon followed by the loss of her ability to reach people who were right there with her.

Though I tried to stay light on my feet, prepared to match any dance (or persona) the music might call for, one mid-December phone call tripped me.

"*Ich hab' Jani verloren. Ich habe überall gesucht und kann sie nicht finden.*" (I've lost Jani. I searched for her everywhere but I can't find her). Throughout her illness Mom had reverted to speaking almost exclusively in German. But that was the first time she referred to me by my childhood name. And it was certainly the first time I heard that she had lost me. I had just spent the afternoon with Mom, and with my seven o'clock good night call I learned that she had been searching for me everywhere. My suggestion that she get ready for her comfortable bed met with resistance. Mom instead insisted she must get off the phone to look for me.

When Ute called Mom moments later for their regular good night call, Jani was still sufficiently lost to Mom's mind that she asked Ute whether she knew where I was. When our phone rang again, I answered it to Ute's concerned greeting. "Chris, could you call Mom and tell her you're alright? She's afraid she's lost you."

My gut churned as I told Ute that Mom had also told me that she couldn't find Jani. How do you put someone at ease who is missing you, if she can't know that you are there with her? Not thinking anything would work, but because I didn't know what else to do, I took another sip of wine and gave myself ten minutes to come up with something brilliant. I couldn't, but called Mom back nevertheless.

When I said tentatively, "Hi Mom," she responded with relief, *"Oh, nun hab Ich Dich endlich gefunden!"* (Oh, I've finally found you!).

I took a deep breath before assuring her, truthfully, that she had indeed found me at home and fine. "Now let's both get into our comfy-cozy beds."

That episode marked the beginning of Mom's looking directly at something but either not seeing it, or not identifying it as what she was seeking. The nightgown search was a case in point.

I first noticed the problem one winter afternoon. All of Mom's laundry had come back to her room clean and folded. I refreshed her bed with bright sheets and hung the huge towel on the rack by her shower. And just so we'd know for sure where it was, we walked to the bathroom door together to hang up Mom's favorite dark blue nightgown. I headed home satisfied that all was in its proper place. But when I called an hour later to say good night, all order had vanished. Mom was convinced she was in the wrong room, and had settled into that (not *her*) bed still wearing her clothes because "she couldn't find her nightgown." For a second I debated whether I should try to guide her to look on the bathroom door. Was it fine for her just to sleep in her dress? It would certainly be easier. But Mom was definitely agitated about her missing nightgown, so I pursued the search. "I think we left it hanging on your bathroom door, Mom. Do you want to check there? I'll stay on the phone."

I heard Mom shuffle off, but then the line was quiet for

so long I began to worry Mom had forgotten that we had been talking. Finally I heard her exasperated, "It isn't there."

"Really?" was all I could come up with. "Your favorite blue nightgown isn't hanging on the door?"

A hollow clunk suggested that Mom had dropped the receiver on her nightstand again and had headed off to continue the search. If I had thought I could reconnect with her, I would have hung up and tried a second call. Then I would have asked more questions rather than trying to help her answer them. But rather than risking an incessant busy signal (who knows when Mom would hang up the phone?), I decided to stay on the line for a bit. After an eternity I heard Mom's heavy breathing with, "Yes, my *nightgown* is there. I just couldn't find what I was looking for because I've never been *here* before."

"But now you've got everything—right?" As she would do more and more over the coming months, I suspected she went back to bed in her dress without changing into the nightgown that represented our much loved "comfy-cozy" time in bed. But once the boundaries between Mom's waking world and her mind's dreams became inseparable, the difference between day and night clothing, too, became irrelevant. "Good night," dear Mom.

WHILE MOM'S FAILING memory was making things more difficult, it also brought unexpected benefits. Mom would accept my explanations and reassurances at face value as the incongruencies between what her mind was perceiving, and what she had formerly known to be reality, had faded. For so long, my eyes, and her own shadowy memory had hinted at the terrible misperceptions of her mind that she could not set straight. As Mom's disease advanced, however, those two worlds became one gray space where all was possible. Earlier, my poor explanations of why we couldn't make that reassuring call to her parents (you remember, they don't have a phone in Dassendorf) distressed Mom. Suddenly, my offers to call her parents later to let them know that she was fine satisfied her. Without a hint of disbelief her unease would dissolve. "Yes, it would be nice if you would do that. I'll sleep here first and go home early tomorrow."

Just how much had changed for all of us became startlingly clear to me when, days before Christmas, with no plans for the festivities, I was trying to ignore the whole blasted affair. Taking Mom out of Mountainview for a change of scenery was no longer a pleasure for anyone. It made Mom terribly anxious to go somewhere with no idea where she was. We'd stopped having meals together at our house, because with every invitation Mom's face turned vacant. "No, I don't know what your house looks like." Or, she'd fret while trying to locate herself. "But where does Paul live?" She'd forgotten that Paul and I were married, so why would we be going to Paul's house rather than "home" for a meal? Why indeed?

Wishing to spare Mom the torment and us the ordeal, part of me wanted to skip Christmas altogether. But I also have some of my grandfather's stubborn streak, and for all that Mom's disease had already taken from us, I was not going to let it claim this traditional source of joy—at least not yet. We ordered a *Turkey in a Box* ("complete traditional dinner with all the fixings including two pies of your choice") and cobbled together a subdued Christmas Eve celebration for all Mom's kids, grand-, and great-grandkids in Mountainview's family room. Not exactly like the holidays I used to cherish, but I could not have been more proud of Ute's grandkids! Briana and Ian seemed to sense that a balance could be struck with honoring their frail, distant great-grandmother observing from the sidelines and their own holiday exuberance.

Although we made no effort to hide the fact that it was Christmas (how could we?), we kept the gift exchange low-key and had no indication whether the tree, lights, cookies, and carols were suggesting Christmas to Mom's mind. We learned, though, when Ute related a conversation she and Mom had had during a quiet moment after dinner while the rest of us were cleaning up. Calmly Mom began, "So, today is Christmas?"

Uncertain where this conversation was going, Ute

134

answered simply, "Yes."

"I don't think I'm ready with presents."

"Oh, don't worry about that Mom. Everything is taken care of. We just wanted to be together."

After a long silence, Mom found her reason for why this Christmas felt so different. "Yes, that was nice. It would all be so much simpler if your father weren't so complicated, wouldn't it?"

Knowing that Dad had found his own peace when he died and wouldn't take offense at being blamed, Ute responded, "Yes, that is true."

In some way it had always been true. Certainly since their divorce, but even in our younger years, Dad's "complicated nature" deeply affected everything we did. It didn't feel strange that it was doing so again.

Together, Curtis and I visited Mom on Christmas Day. I brought along Mom's favorites, eggnog and homemade rumballs, for some cheer. Unwrapped, so it wouldn't remind Mom

Mom's first day of school, 1930

of presents she didn't have for others, I also brought a photo scrapbook I'd prepared as a gift. The first page showed Mom and Dad as infants in the 1920s. By decade and event, the pages scrolled through their love and life until their grandchildren were shown in their junior high years. The album ended in the late 1970s, before Dad left the pictures—and our lives. Mom was delighted with every turn of the page and pointed, as if spotting a long-lost friend, to each of her childhood pictures with an elated, "...and that's *me!*"

Curtis and I enjoyed the album, too—at least as much as we cherished that time of watching Mom's memories flow, edited and truncated, but freely. Then Curtis went to visit his father's family and he left Mom and me basking in the glow of how well Curtis was doing. "I like how we smile at each other," Mom beamed, and I fought off a wave of melancholy as Mom's eyes turned thoughtful.

Absentmindedly she turned the album pages again until she settled on a photograph of her three grandchildren, eight and ten years old, smiling broadly at the camera at one of the many family gatherings Mom had hosted. Concentrating fiercely, Mom looked long and hard at the picture before she expressed her confusion, "And do you know where all those kids are now?"

Although Michael, Debi, and Curtis had all matured over the intervening thirty years, they remained to my eyes unmistakably the same "kids." Mom, however, had spent the past twenty-four hours close to each one and yet did not recognize them in the picture. What was there to say except the truth? "They all grew up, Mom. And they are doing just fine!"

"Well, isn't that nice. Then everyone's okay, aren't they?"

"Oh yes, dear Mom." Grateful that I could feel the warmth of her tender hands in mine, I turned my face away to swallow the tears. "Everyone really *is* fine." Merry Christmas!

Fading into Night: 2005

"Wisdom consists not so much in knowing what to do
in the ultimate as in knowing what to do next."
–Herbert Hoover

OTHER THAN THAT, Mrs. Lincoln how did you enjoy the play?
Illustrating the absurdity of totally misjudging the gravity of a
situation, that silly saying crossed my mind whenever a well-
meaning listener would respond to my summary of how Mom's
dementia was affecting our lives by asking, "But is she in good
health otherwise?"

I understood the hopeful intention and unspoken assumption of the question. At least it wasn't heart failure, or liver
cancer, or some other life-threatening ailment—right? But
it was painful to be repeatedly reminded that the degree of
Mom's distress, for not being more physical, I supposed, was
so poorly understood. If the song has stated for years that *the
knee bone's connected to the thigh bone*, why could people who
were kind enough to ask about Mom not know that, in one
body, there *is* no otherwise. No, she is not okay—even otherwise, was my invariable inner response preceding my polite
words. "She has a terrible disease that changes everything
about her health."

So, while maybe in degree, certainly in kind there was
nothing strikingly different in Mom's illness that Christmas of
2004. That she did not recognize in the pictures of her young
grandchildren the same adults with whom she had just spent
the holidays was simply another loss along a steady continuum
of mental deterioration. By early 2005, however, Mom's body
was also visibly beginning to break down. If I didn't mention

Mom's physical ailments yet when asked about her condition, I could have recited a litany of physical afflictions both caused and exacerbated by the fact that Mom's brain was no longer functioning properly.

Occasional incontinence is not unusual in the elderly, especially with women whose reproductive tissues have been robbed of elasticity by their bearing children. Most residents at Mountainview wore some kind of protective underwear to guard against "accidents." But early in that new year it became obvious that for Mom there was no longer anything accidental about not making it to the bathroom in time. She had not recognized for quite some time her brain's poorly transmitted messages that she needed to empty her bladder.

It had increasingly become Mom's habit to stay in bed and "rest up"—all day. Friends had commented that her ultra-polite sense of hospitality was giving way to weary resignation. She no longer insisted on getting up to greet visitors or walking them to the door when they left. For that matter, she no longer insisted on walking at all. Rather than having to search for Mom in the activities area or at a table in another house, when I arrived on those winter afternoons I would find her in bed. She was always pleased to see me, but after a short greeting Mom would return her focus to somewhere in space. After trying for a long time to sort out her restless confusion, Mom would settle on the familiar theme. "I'm waiting for my Mum." She kept staring longingly into nowhere muttering absentmindedly, "My Mum said she would be here at four today."

I had said that, too, I would think sadly while searching for a way to excuse why her Mum hadn't made it once again. With Colorado's brilliant winter sunshine and temperatures in the sixties, it was not easy to blame the weather, but that didn't keep me from trying. "It's still January, Mom. And it gets dark early. You always said your Mum isn't very strong, and she probably knew better than to take on that long journey today."

While that tactic often worked—Mom would shift mental gears to the days when she helped her Mum carry groceries on their walks to Dassendorf—there was that day when nothing

138

I could say moved Mom. She was so obviously unconvinced by my explanation that I switched to distractions. "Maybe you would like to go for a short walk before dinner?"

Suddenly alert, Mom's response was immediate. Her "No" was so adamant that I started to probe. "Are you feeling okay? Does anything hurt?"

Instead of Mom's usual, practiced repetition of, "Oh yes, I'm very comfortable. No, nothing hurts," this time she hesitated and stuttered. "Yes, something hurts."

I figured that Mom's muscles must ache and still believed this was the same ailment that had been keeping her from wanting to be up and walking.

"Oh, I'm sorry. Are your legs sore?"

"Yes, between my legs."

A little puzzled, I pointed to my knees, thighs, and hips, "Here? Here?"

"At the top," she mumbled pointing to her groin.

Her underwear must be really wet and clammy I thought. And since it was always a relief to be of some practical help I gladly jumped at the opportunity to *do* something, "Oh well, we can fix that. Why don't we get you into the bathroom and get dry panties on?"

"No, I'm too tired. I don't want to do that now."

Mom's discomfort was obvious, though, and I persisted as she painfully wriggled under the covers. "What if I help you here in the bed?"

Her resistance weakened, but she wasn't ready to relent. "You don't need to. I can take care of it myself. I'm just too lazy."

That made me angry. Not at Mom, but at this whole mess! I hated it when she blamed herself for her situation. Mom, on the other hand, did not seem upset by her explanation, and looking back, I wonder whether it gave her some sense of control to simply *choose* not to do anything about her difficulties rather than admit that she couldn't.

"Why don't we just try to do something here so you don't hurt so much, though?" Without waiting for an answer I gently moved my hands under the covers and we talked calmly as I tussled with the three soggy pairs of padded panties she was wearing. Three, I wondered? Mom must have never taken the soiled pair off and had just put another on each time she thought she needed a change. Regardless, they were all drenched with urine and the elastic leg-closures had dug angry welts into her flesh. Pulling the soaked lump away and over Mom's hips was a struggle. When I finally succeeded, the acid stench stung my nostrils as I walked the few steps to the bathroom and unceremoniously dumped the heavy mass into the sink. I poured on far more detergent than necessary, but no more than my sensibilities needed to dispel my disgust. When did this situation get bad enough to literally reek of gross negligence?

Back beside Mom in her bed, I draped a towel across her lap and offered, "Why don't I bring you a warm, wet washcloth and you can wash yourself really well down there?"

"I don't have any warm water here," she absent-mindedly responded.

I'd already turned the shower on for the hottest water possible; and with barely enough time to offer, "Let me just check it out," I was back with that warm, wet washcloth. Mom began to clean herself vigorously and finally admitted relief. "That feels *so* good." Mom thanked me profusely each time she handed me the cloth to be refreshed. She did not seem to notice what I saw with some alarm, that it was blood-stained every time Mom passed it back to me. After four or five washes Mom was ready to dry herself.

With her still under the towel, I was anxious to know where the blood was coming from. But how could I ask Mom to permit me such an invasion of her privacy? Better to ask forgiveness later than be refused now, I reasoned, and craned my neck to sneak a peak at the affected area before sliding up dry underwear. I needn't have worried. Mom did not resist my inspection and sores festering on the insides of Mom's thighs and labia were very visible. "My God, yes, that would hurt!" Appalled, I gently closed Mom's legs to recover from that dreadful sight. "I think I'll ask the nurse for some lotion, Mom; I'll be right back." Mom smiled agreeably, but assured me that already her legs no longer hurt.

More attention to Mom's hygiene had been promised at our last care-conference, and the nurse on duty at Mountainview that day confirmed that the caregivers had indeed been reminding Mom to use the bathroom every few hours. However, she added defensively, Mom often insisted that she didn't need to go. Furthermore, I understood all too well the staff's reluctance to force themselves into Mom's very personal space. I hadn't meant for my distress at Mom's condition to color my tone as I asked for some lotion. I really wasn't blaming anyone—it was just the whole, horrible situation.

"But other than that...," I grumbled sarcastically to myself before returning to Mom armed with diaper rash ointment. She didn't hesitate when I asked to apply some to her "sore legs," and it must have been very comforting to have me spread the thick salve that would protect Mom's raw, sensitive skin from urine burns. I finished our chore with a dousing of baby powder before pulling on her single dry pair of panties.

Mom never again resisted our daily "panty routine" as long as we used *Penaten Crème*, the traditional German skin protector Mom had used on our baby bottoms. I had to order the salve from a Canadian pharmacy, but it was well worth it. An unused tin still sits on my dresser. I open it occasionally just to breathe in the distinctive sweet scent that reminds me of a dry, clean baby—and those intimate moments with Mom.

But that first time we were simply glad to have the ordeal behind us. We were also exhausted, however, by the effort to alleviate what could only have been painful for Mom. For me it was at least as hard to see Mom's injury, and then to invade her most intimate body-area. Words inadequate, all we could manage was to rest limply together on Mom's bed. She was lying down, "comfy-cozy," while I sat close. We simply held hands, recovering as dusk with an early-setting January sun slowly darkened the room. Once Mom had closed her eyes, her fingers started to play some unsung tune on my knuckles.

Suddenly Mom raised her head and seized my eyes with hers. Steadily she studied my expression, before a child's smile of recognition slid across her face. "Oh, I didn't think you were still going to come today. I was so afraid I wasn't going to *see* you today."

Her eyes were already closed again, but her smile remained as I reminded her, "Oh no, dear Mom, you can never get away from me. I'll always come and find you!"

"That's good. Chrissie tells me that, too!"

I acknowledged her contentment by stroking her arm.

Finally, after this long, strenuous time, for one blessed moment my beloved Mom had been afforded that bone-deep comfort only a present, loving mother can provide—or a daughter. Because, whoever she was becoming, at that moment she wasn't longing for some other, *after-this-life* home. She simply experienced the grace of physical comfort, mental ease, and tactile pleasure. We kept touching, carefully *covering*, as Curtis had advised years earlier, a moment I knew would pass all too quickly. But one in which Mom had found her Mum holding her hand—just as I was holding the hands of mine.

AS THE DAYS grew sunnier and warmer, Mom's skin started to break down. Or more accurately, Mom started scratching at herself. Everything itched. Some combination of dry, fragile skin, boredom, anxiety, and topical irritation conspired to make any spot Mom could reach fair game. Even short, neatly filed nails were destructive enough to turn Mom's body into a quilt of angry sores. They turned me into a wreck.

Now that Mom was spending so much time in bed, the sharp edges of her favorite coral necklace (a purchase she had proudly made from a Navajo artist on her retirement trip to the American Southwest) were irritating her neck as it was resting against the pillow all day. It made sense that Mom should be scratching there. But it wasn't clear why Mom continued long after the offending piece had been removed and forgotten in her jewelry box.

Craving warmth as much as she did, Mom was often bundled into her hand-knitted sweaters, and we thought the salty sweat under the rough fabric might surely be causing her itching. But even after switching to soft fleece for warmth, Mom would absentmindedly, and vigorously, tear at herself. We tried to soothe her skin by liberally applying every conceivable lotion: "Hypoallergenic," "For dry, itchy skin," "For sensitive skin," "Super-moisturizing." There was no limit to the manufacturers' claims, but none to Mom's distress either. We banished even the mildest soaps and body washes, rinsing Mom with warm water, and started washing her clothes and bedding with baby detergent. In spite of our efforts, as soon as Mom's neck would heal there'd be new welts on her breasts. If she was wearing long-sleeved blouses to protect her arms, she'd distractedly reach for her belly. And while sitting in Activities where we had hoped singing or drawing would keep her mind on something else, her hands would wander down to claw at her legs. Nothing any of us knew to do would help.

When I could no longer tolerate Mom's distress, I made an appointment for her with a dermatologist. I didn't do it lightly. Mom had last been outside Mountainview eight months earlier to attend my "non-birthday" party at Jen's house. Unable to locate herself in what was by then a completely foreign environment, she had been terribly anxious. A visit to the doctor had never been anyone's idea of an enjoyable outing. By now, just leaving the relative familiarity of Mom's four walls had become a frightening ordeal for her. But we really had no choice. We had to see a specialist before any relief could be prescribed. So off we went.

Mom held up remarkably well. With obviously no idea where she was, she took each new view of the mountains with pleasant surprise and was her usual compliant self with the young physician. The visit was brief and inconclusive. "Unfortunately," was the doctor's guarded observation, "your Mom's skin condition is not an unusual one in the elderly."

I was sick and tired of hearing yet again what degree of discomfort was considered tolerable, or essentially untreatable, in dementia sufferers. I nodded silently. I had long ago accepted losing the war and had held out little hope of winning this skin battle; there was no magic bullet. But the physician did supply some ammunition. We left armed with a steroid ointment for the "affected areas" and a sedative to be given "as needed." At least we had something.

The confusion of the morning didn't really hit Mom until we were having lunch in her room. "I can't stay here. I've never been here before." Mom's agitated mind was racing to impose some order on the chaos around her. "They don't know me here. I have to watch for the bus to get home."

I pointed out that she was in *her* bed. The phone on which Ute and I called every evening to say "night-night" was right there beside her. "And look, on that wall across from you is the picture of your Mum."

"Yes. But this isn't *my* room. When is the bus leaving?" All the while, Mom was methodically ripping the scabs off the scratches healing on her arm.

Maybe that sedative wasn't such a bad idea. I asked the Mountainview nurse whether this might be a good time to give Mom an anti-itch pill. Of course. Promising that this would make her feel better, I handed Mom the medication with some water and applied another layer of steroid ointment to her worst sores. Mom became noticeably calmer. She slid progressively further down among her pillows as her drooping eyelids finally brought some rest. But even this strong medication couldn't right what was unalterably wrong. "You'll tell me when the bus comes—right? You won't leave me in this place!"

Squeezing her hands gently, and finding no other way to hide that I would do precisely that, I lied. "You can sleep Mom, I'll be sure to let you know when it's time to go."

Throughout the afternoon I tried to call Mom to see how she was doing, but her phone just rang and rang. Finally, when I still couldn't reach her for our good night routine, I called Mountainview. The *Santa Fe House* caregiver assured me Mom was fine. She had been sleeping soundly for hours, and would continue to do so throughout the night. By the next morning, Mom had forgotten all about being in the wrong room and was glad for her good sleep in *her* comfy-cozy bed. The sedative had helped after all.

While Mountainview was the right living situation for

Mom at that stage of her life, her skin troubles revealed a disadvantage of not having her in a skilled nursing facility. Since two medications were to be used "as required," rather than on a regular schedule, constant monitoring of Mom's nervous energy and comfort level was necessary to evaluate whether and where the steroid ointment should be applied. Even while I sat with Mom in the afternoons, her hands would seek somewhere to scratch to relieve the itching. Then her fingers would work so quickly and vigorously that she would create a new "affected area" on some part of her body before even I had time to intervene. If I couldn't stop it while sitting beside her, I knew the caregivers could not do so by occasionally checking on Mom.

More difficult yet were decisions about the anti-itch tablet. The caregivers could not make a medical judgment on whether, at any given moment, Mom's condition warranted something—a regulated substance that would make her groggy—to relieve her distress. Mom's condition first needed to be observed and then judged severe enough by someone who would decide whether it warranted involving the nurse. Mountainview's nursing staff, however, had forty-five other charges, so they were not always instantly available to be asked about giving Mom the pill. It meant, further, that whoever gave Mom the medication had to be aware of and available to deal with the effects—intended and otherwise—of the medication.

Mom's sleepiness from the pill was expected. In fact, we thought she deserved the rest from her discomfort. Unfortunately, the drug can also cause diarrhea, a mighty inconvenient side effect for one no longer able to identify the body's signals and respond quickly.

The first *disaster*, and this was Mom's word, was just that. My knock on Mom's door that afternoon went unanswered long enough to lead me to think Mom was having a better day. Maybe I'd find her at the daily Activities period. When I didn't, I returned to her room, knocked again, and after a period of silence from Mom's side of the door, let myself in. "Hi, Mom; it's just me. Are you alright?"

I hadn't even opened the door wide enough to see Mom,

mortified, lying in bed, when I was assaulted by a terrific stench. "Something has happened."

Right! "Are you feeling alright, Mom? Did you get sick?"

"Oh no, I'm fine. But there has been a disaster."

Right again. There were feces everywhere. I found stool material on floors and walls, surrounding the toilet, and covering Mom's body, clothes, and bedding. As unbelievable as the whole scene was, Mom's explanation was even more so. By her recollection, she needed to leave her "class" in a hurry for the bathroom. But when she got to her room, she met with this *disaster.*

"Really, and you're feeling well? Your stomach doesn't hurt?"

"No, I don't know who got in here to make this mess."

"Well, as long as you're okay, let's just clean this up."

Easier said than done, but I did get it done, that time and the others that followed. Mom never again explained these occurrences in terms of an intruder, but I almost wished she would have. It was much harder to put her through the humiliation of the cleaning process while she was agonizing, "Did *I* poop all over the place?"

Whatever good the occasional anti-itch pill might have been doing keeping Mom comfortable without constant drowsiness, it was not worth this price! Mountainview's staff and washing machines worked overtime; I was running out of clean, dry blankets and good will; and Mom was reduced to only occasional, sad comments. "With poop in my bed, what would I have done if you hadn't come?"

Not entirely convinced, I nevertheless tried to respond lightly. "Well, dear Mom, good thing we don't need to worry about that! I'll always find you!"

Mom's "Continuing Care" physician's assistant agreed that it might be best to put her on a regular low dose of the anti-itch medication. Her body adjusted to that lower but more constant level of medication so that over time the sleepiness subsided somewhat and the *disasters* were fewer. True, the bad side effects of the medication were less pronounced, but so was everything else that Mom needed to function. Every aspect of her life had been muted. By the time the autumn colors gave way to bare trees lining my drive to Mountainview, and the nights got cold enough so the back-range of the Rockies kept that initial dusting of snow, some of the collateral damage of Mom's disease had been eliminated. But so had all the other feelings and reactions that might have given Mom a life we would consider worth living.

THE PREVIOUS CHRISTMAS, almost a year ago, I had given Mom a calendar with a different family picture as the theme for each month. For June I had chosen a picture of Curtis. In July, Mike and Mom's great-grand-kids were laughing

Ute and her beloved Winston taking a September birthday walk on their favorite Oregon beach, September 2005.

over a backyard picnic. August, with summer always refer-ring back to Maine, showed an earlier photo of Mom sitting on our deck overlooking Pigeon Hill Bay, and for December (what else?) a family photo of everyone around the decorated Christ-mas dinner table of years ago. Mom never made the connection between the photograph and the month chosen to relate birth-days and special events to times of the year. But she generally enjoyed seeing the family pictures from her bed.

The November page, however, was a flop. Several years earlier, Paul and I had purchased a VW camper and in October had taken it on its maiden voyage to Yellowstone National Park. It had been a memorable trip, both for the pleasure of traveling in our new acquisition, and for spectacular Yellow-stone. On a stone outcropping in front of Yellowstone Falls, clad in parkas against the early morning chill and wearing broad-brimmed hats to protect against the sun, Paul and I posed for the obligatory picture another visitor offered to take. The camera captured the colorful autumn leaves clinging to the sides of a steep canyon, and the silver water plunging into a pool far below where we stood smiling in a close embrace. True, everything there is on a grand scale, and our figures are dwarfed by Nature in the photograph. But it showed clearly that Paul and I were having a marvelous morning.

With no hint that my birthday month might have a picture of me, Mom didn't recognize me when I turned to the November page. Perplexed she stared at the calendar. "Who is that old lady with Paul?"

I laughed and agreed that, yes, with that funny hat I was kind of hard to recognize. Frustrated, Mom just got more insistent. Of course she saw me, but who was that old lady? Since Paul and I were the only people in the photo it stumped us where in the scene Mom saw me and who she thought was "that old lady." But whatever Mom saw in that image remained so upsetting to her that by the second week in November I had turned the calendar back to a more comfortable picture. The months didn't matter anyway. The date cheerfully claiming it was February (with a close-up picture of Paul and me in a Valentine heart) did not contradict my telling Mom on the third Wednesday of November that Paul, Curtis, and I were looking forward to celebrating the Mountainview Family Thanksgiving with her the next day. Mom nodded contentedly, but became thoughtful as she scowled at the calendar on the wall. "But tell Paul not to bring that old lady."

I never learned what generated those feelings in either the picture or Mom's mind, but I simply laughed and bent to hug her. "Right, Mom, I'll make sure Paul brings me."

There were many days throughout that year when I couldn't face going to Mountainview. Moments when the sights, sounds and smells of finding Mom there were unbearable, and the thought of leaving her there yet another day heartbreaking. But at no time did I not want to see my Mom. So I went, and never tired of being greeted by the residents' various pets. Jewel's favorite place was in her owner's lap, perfectly pleased to watch her small world in Mountainview's hallways go round and round while Jean shuffled her feet slowly to scoot their wheelchair forward. But as soon as I came through the door, she'd launch herself off her throne, lick any part of me she could reach, and quickly jump back to safety, all the while yipping the good news that a visitor had arrived. Older than Jewel and half-blind, Emily was less agile but no less enthusiastic. In trusting adoration she presented herself, belly-up and tail wagging as vigorously as her arthritic hips allowed, for an elaborate, tummy-rubbing welcome.

My favorite, though, was Millie. True to her Australian Shepherd breeding, she was more reserved. It wouldn't do, she seemed to think, to abandon one's dignity over just anybody. So she would sit with every muscle taut at the end of the hall until you broke the ice. "Aw, come on Millie, you know me...." Properly introduced, she'd accept you as a friend, glue her head to your legs for a thorough ear-scratching, and follow you everywhere with her Frisbee. She would sneak into Mom's room right on my heels, plop herself next to Mom on the bed and patiently receive Mom's gentle petting. Her soft coat and sweet nature were solace for Mom's hands and soul.

Millie's owner, Eleanor, had been Mom's neighbor and tablemate. And although I know that at least three Mountainview residents, including Mom, claimed Millie as their own, Millie herself was never confused about her ultimate loyalty. She was her owner's family and life-support, and no one was surprised to see less of Millie after Eleanor fell and broke her hip. Like the faithful friend she was, Millie remained by Eleanor's bed constantly and came from her room, downcast and all business, only when she absolutely needed to be let outside. I missed seeing her sensible, loving heart around *Santa Fe House*, but I reminded myself that she was close by and precisely where she needed to be.

My knowledge of Millie's devotion notwithstanding, I wasn't prepared for our sad reunion the afternoon Millie was once again lying in the dining room. She didn't raise an eyebrow at my joyous, "Sweet Millie, I'm so glad to see you!" So, I got down on my knees to meet her unresponsive gaze and scratch those silky ears. We both knew Eleanor had died, and I rested my forehead on Millie's chest to cry. The sadness I felt at both Millie's loss of her beloved mistress and our own loss of Millie's spirit was all-consuming. I do remember, though, huddled on the floor into that grief-stricken softness Mom so loved, that I caught the flicker of Christmas lights blinking in the corner of the room. And I thought bitterly what an utterly appropriate way this was to cap a miserable year. "But other than *that....*"

End of the Rainbow: Winter-Spring 2006

"The world is not to be put in order. The world is in order.
It is for us to put ourselves in unison with this order."
–Henry Miller

THERE WERE STILL folks at Mountainview pacing the halls in the same methodical way they did when Mom moved in two years earlier. But the passage of time had taken its toll, and the disease from which the residents suffered had changed the community noticeably. Some had retreated into their own world, one which we could not enter and from which we could not retrieve them; some had to be moved to hospital care or skilled nursing facilities; and others had died in their rooms at Mountainview. Watching the slow decline of Mom's neighbors, I dreaded seeing yet another nameplate disappear from a door almost as much as I loathed watching the deterioration of those left behind.

And I started to do the math. The *average* stay at Mountainview was "about three years." One of Mom's neighbors, who had become as much of a friend as was possible in a community of people who couldn't remember the face they saw minutes earlier, had fallen after just a few months at Mountainview. She died less than a week after that accident. But for everyone at the low end of that average, I knew there had to be someone staying alive twice as long to derive the average.

Regardless of the number of days and months Mom would reside at Mountainview, "Alive in all Seasons of Life" was the motto we gladly accepted when we chose it as the right place for her. Structured and supervised group activities, her own space, and very little that betrayed institutional living for the residents, combined with the availability of caring help when needed, confirmed for us that Mom would live as good a life as possible throughout her illness. But the disease process is ruthless, and trying to figure out just how to define *quality of life* given Mom's suffering was not easy.

Come spring, I'd catch myself nodding ambivalent agreement when one of the caregivers would triumphantly announce that they had been able to get Mom interested in attending an activity that day. True, it was impossible not to smile when I caught her fingers tapping to the rhythm of *You Are My Sunshine* even before I'd see her face brighten at my arrival. What's not to enjoy when Mom was out having a better day! It was no less of a relief, however, to find Mom comfortably snuggled in her bed, unwilling to get up, "just," as she would always say, "resting all day."

Convinced she deserved that rest, I read German magazines to her and fed Mom her favorite yogurt and bananas rather than rouse her to join the group in the dining room for meals. I then thankfully accepted the reprieve of our good night kiss with her assurance that, "Oh yes, I'm always comfortable in my bed." On those nights I knew Mom would not have to struggle with trying to rise from the table after meals having no idea where her room might be, and worse, completely unsure whether her legs would actually get her there once someone helped her figure it out.

"Just rest, dear Mom," I'd say, welcoming anything that would keep her mind and body at ease, and yes, *alive* in this last stage of her life. Because in our minds, dying—and she was dying—may be the final but no less natural season of life.

Whatever else my Mom had been, she was never average. Still, as we rolled into our third year of Mom's stay at Mountainview, I somehow knew that this would also be her last. By the winter of 2005, Mom's strength was waning and her inability to connect with much of anything around her forced us to acknowledge that we'd celebrated our last holiday season together. Mom was letting go. She had lived honorably and graciously, respecting life above all. But Mom had been nothing if not pragmatic. Hers had never been some distant, romantic notion of life. She was used to instantly translating any need she saw into the responsible action to relieve it. For eight decades she had worked and willed herself to do right for those around her. What Mom couldn't bear was being denied the ability to live by her exacting standard. It became more and more obvious to us that she was preparing to leave this life—maybe even by choice. Taking my cues from her as I had done for over fifty years, I watched. And I reluctantly agreed to abide by her rules.

Oh, there were still good moments, very good ones. I've rarely been happier than on January 6 (I remember because it was Epiphany) when Millie again met me at the entrance of *Santa Fe House.* Upright with her ears cocked and her eyes bright, she quivered with expectation before bounding toward me at my pleased, "Sweet Millie, come say Hi to me!" As Eleanor's family was not able to care for Millie, the Mountainview staff had accepted her as the honorary "house dog," a decision made possible when one of the nurses offered to adopt her. When she wasn't at work, Elena took Millie home to let her run off the extra pounds she'd put on from munching on the treats waiting for her under the table from all the residents who claimed her as their own. But Elena brought Millie back any time she was on duty, and this allowed all of us who had grown to love Millie to keep her in our lives—and on Mom's bed!

In February, our dear friend, the world-renowned Gospel musician Dr. Horace Clarence Boyer, made another

visit to Mountainview to honor Mom and the other residents with his voice and spirit. Mom could not respond verbally when Horace asked whether she had a favorite piece she'd like him to share. But as soon as he rolled his hands across the piano keys and his rich voice proclaimed, "There *is* a Balm in Gilead," Mom's index finger slid lightly back and forth on the arm of her chair. Her rhythm and tempo were flawlessly exact, and the warm softness of her face betrayed joys in some way remembered and deeply felt, if not identified.

Somewhere along the way Curtis had decided to nurture the musical talent he had inherited from his grandparents and had become more diligent with his guitar playing. He was taking lessons, and his spending the required practice hours playing and singing for his Omi became a favorite pastime throughout the spring. Curtis would strum, we would sing, and regardless of how many times we repeated a tune, at the end of every song Mom would raise her slender hands from the bed and vigorously clap them in delight. No matter how far into her own world she had withdrawn during our little performance, as soon as we began "Swing Low, Sweet Chariot," Mom would rouse herself to sing along.

That April, Mountainview had an art show. The program, encouraging the residents to combine art with their personal memories, had produced several interesting pieces that were submitted to the national Alzheimer's Association for regional display. Mom's "The Farms" was among those chosen. The artistry of Mountainview's residents was celebrated with a wine and cheese reception, a lovely effort to honor the artists. Mingling with the other families and proudly commenting on the many interesting paintings, we wandered through the exhibit with Paul and Curtis each tucked into Mom supporting an elbow. They were effectively carrying her.

Thus fully occupied, and with plenty on our minds, one drawing still stood out as remarkable. A gentleman who had been a professional artist before he became ill had drawn it. This recent work hung surrounded by his earlier beautifully rendered images of the West: mountains, horses, and an evening on a cattle drive with a pot of beans over the campfire, spurs cast aside for the evening, and the saddle on the ground poised for nighttime duty as a pillow. Without this display, no one would have guessed that those earlier paintings and the recent one with its simple brushstrokes of a stick figure with a huge hat, some kind of ring next to it, and a large black scribble in a corner were by the same hand. But there was no question that both came from the same heart. Appropriately, the Mountainview artist had titled his most recent drawing "Cowboy, Donut and Bird."

Mom seemed exhausted and overwhelmed throughout the event, and no matter how much she enjoyed being surrounded by "Chrissie's men," she could only remain on her feet for a very few minutes at a time. And why bother? She genuinely had no idea what the fuss was about when it came to the display of her work. "What, *I* did that?" She was incredulous.

"The Farms" Ilse Waengler

It was impossible to tell what she might have felt or wanted to express with her picture of a house with lots of trees and a smiling man and woman in each corner. Is this the Dassendorf and her parents she's been longing to go home to? Only the barely visible *Ilse Wängler* scrawled in one corner of the page told us that we were looking at a reflection of Mom's soul, whether memory of the past or hope for the future.

There were good moments, to be sure, but Mountainview's Annual Mother's Day Tea passed unnoticed. Despite the unseasonably hot day in May, Mom was firmly ensconced in a mountain of pillows and blankets when I arrived. It was clear that it made no sense to coax her to participate in the festivities. In other years, I know she would have enjoyed the music and her perennial favorite, a piece of cheesecake. But this was now; and as far as I could tell Mom heard little of my stories and took no notice of the big bunch of flowers Ute and I had brought for her. No matter how I tried to reach her, nothing seemed to connect us.

When I visited the following day, things were completely different. Stepping lightly to the unpredictable tune of this disease, I immediately shifted into Mom's relatively upbeat mood. Although in bed as usual, Mom noticed the brilliant sun coming through her window and nodded willingness when I suggested we go outside for a bit. Initially she gazed at her helpless legs, but when I assured her I could find a wheelchair and she wouldn't have to walk, her demeanor brightened. If it didn't rise to the level of her former eagerness to get outside, Mom certainly showed more than a passive readiness. Once in the garden, we commented on the bees and flowers and were enchanted by a baby rabbit so tame it barely hopped out of our path.

Mom's beautiful, fragile hands impressed me almost as much. With paper-thin skin now taut across arthritic bones that used to be strong enough to make music with a bow gliding over strings of catgut, Mom's fingers lay spread out on the arm of the wheelchair. They seemed to be yearning to absorb the sun, not only as it warmed the skin at that moment, but also to capture permanently the heat Mom now so craved.

Though only a few minutes passed before Mom grew tired and wanted to return to her bed, our moments in the fresh air had awakened something in her and produced a glimmer of what had so often happened between us in the past. As soon as we got back to her room, Mom even commented on the Mother's Day flowers by her bed. Whether she had seen them before or not, she was obviously noticing them for the first time.

"They are lovely," she mused. But my satisfaction was short-lived, as they did not have the effect Ute and I had wished. "Why didn't those flowers go to my Mum?" Mom became immediately self-critical. "They were supposed to go to Dassendorf."

I was amazed that some Mother's Day reference had penetrated Mom's consciousness after all, but saddened that she didn't know herself as the one deserving the flowers. "Ute and I wanted you to have a Mother's Day treat, too." But I countered Mom's scolding herself only once as it became increasingly stressful for her to look at the bouquet. Each time her eyes caught sight of it, she would reprimand herself for not having gotten the flowers to her Mum. Finally, I moved the vase by the door where she could no longer see it, and promised to make sure her Mum received the bouquet.

"Can you do that?" she asked with obvious relief.

"Oh, sure Mom, I can do that." Before I completed my outrageous claim, Mom was already settling into a calm sleep.

There wasn't much that surprised me anymore in either the way Mom's disease showed in her behavior and perceptions or my reaction to it. I'd grown adept at traveling across the gaping chasms separating our worlds, and avoided analyzing at which point my lies crossed over them to become our truths. As long as Mom's reassuring smile met me on the other side, all that mattered was that she was satisfied and at peace. Once Mom was asleep, however, leaving me to straddle the gaps alone, I was beset by doubt and loneliness. My words rang hollow in my ears, "Oh sure, I could *really* get flowers to my long departed grandmother."

Perhaps it was the recognition of the absurdity of my casually offered reassurance. Or maybe it was my own near belief that my grandmother would be able to sense my loving intent, if only the limiting definitions of life and death could be stretched far enough. But I ached with sadness as I sneaked the offending flowers out of the room, doing so to deliver them "on Mom's behalf" to her Mum. What the hell was I thinking of to make such a promise? How on earth could I not make it?

When Mom woke up, we were both in better spirits. The first bites of that evening's peach yogurt seemed especially delicious, but after only a few spoonfuls Mom was ready to go back to sleep. I hugged her tightly before saying good night and was already in the doorway when Mom waved to me from below her covers grinning at something she remembered. "When you see your father, whack him in the head."

I laughed and nodded my head. "You bet, Mom, when I see Dad I'll do just that!" They would both deserve that expression of the anger Mom had held silently for over two decades I thought as I headed to the car. Wedging the vase of flowers I would leave on our dining room table (rather than with my grandmother) between the seat and the seatbelt, I chuckled again before driving home through a veil of tears.

Regardless of moments of personal closeness with me and the effort of the Mountainview activities director to engage Mom, she continued her withdrawal from us. She rarely left her bed anymore, preferring to have me help her eat a few swallows of something light there rather than getting up to join the group in the dining room. For hours her eyes would be either closed or vaguely focused on something I had no hope of seeing even though I was looking at exactly the same spot on the wall. And believe me, I tried. I knew well that Mom's increasing detachment from the things I could easily see not only signaled but also hastened the beginning of the end for her. In a vicious spiral of decline, we understood that the less Mom could do, the less she would be able to do. As weak as her legs were, if she didn't move them at all, muscle atrophy would soon render them completely useless. And if she stopped having any social interaction by constantly staying in bed, her few remaining moments of lucidity would also soon disappear in total isolation.

THEN MOM STARTED falling. The first time, we thought it might not have been an actual fall. A caregiver had been walking with Mom when something sort of *gave way* and she slid down. Unable to keep Mom from going completely to the ground—no one, we knew, could stop an adult's uninterrupted fall—we were still grateful that someone had been with her to ease her landing. There were several more close calls as she lost her strength and threatened to go down. One morning in early May, a caregiver found Mom on the floor of her room unable to get up. No one, least of all Mom herself, knew how long she had been there.

We were all relieved that it wasn't worse. She hadn't broken anything after all; but the upset of the incident was obviously still with Mom when I got to Mountainview an hour later. The caregivers had not wanted to leave her in bed alone, so I found her sitting forlornly in a wheelchair at a dining room table. For all it forgets within minutes or seconds of an occurrence, why does her mind have to hang on to this humiliation, I fumed to myself? Bruised and exhausted, all Mom really wanted was to get out of the dining room back into her own bed. And all I really wanted was to make so reasonable a desire possible for her. Still, having to get her only inches from wheelchair to bed, I was overwhelmed by the immensity of the task. I was terrified to move Mom who simply could not support herself. She could not even figure out how to move her feet once standing. But we had to try.

With the wheelchair as close as possible to Mom's bed, we first talked through the tasks ahead of us. First, Mom needed to set her feet down and rise from the chair. Determination temporarily allowed her to support her weight as she stood precariously suspended above the seat. Facing her, I held her upper body with her arms fiercely grasping my neck and shoulders. Not too stable, I worried, but I could quickly give the wheelchair a short shove with my foot to get it out of the way. Then all we needed was a quarter body turn followed by only the smallest pivot on her feet to land her safely in bed. I half heaved, half guided Mom's hips past the armrests on the chair, using one foot to jostle it a few inches back. Mom clung to me heavily, but steadily. We'd almost made it!

Then it all came to a halt. As we desperately clutched each other, Mom fixed those unknowing eyes squarely on me and asked, "*Und was soll ich jetzt tun?*" Her exasperated question, "and what am I supposed to do now?" pointed to yet another consequence of Mom's disease. She was receiving no cues from her brain as to how to scoot her foot just a few degrees to sit on the bed. With all my limbs fully engaged in the wrestling hold we had on each other, I frantically tried to figure out how to bring the wheelchair back beneath Mom and, if I could manage that, let her drop back into it. But that was a big IF. Besides, I reminded myself, the wheelchair was the one place she did not want to be. So I swallowed my panic and slowly slid one hand off her hip down onto Mom's leg, all the while pushing it and urging her to move *that* leg over just a bit. When we couldn't hold our position any longer and Mom sank deeper in my arms, I had no idea whether we had managed a turn sufficient to land her safely, or whether she would slide down to the floor again.

By some stroke of luck (I thought we were due one) Mom's backside caught the edge of the bed. Barely, but it was enough. Somehow we got her scooted over and comfortably settled into her one last refuge. When I finally allowed myself to breathe, I leaned over and held her. "Oh Mom, I'm so sorry you fell and had to wait on the floor to get help." Always the stoic, she lifted the corners of her mouth as her eyes took on that familiar smile. The ordeal, she insisted, hadn't been *that* bad, "although (now her face in a full grin) the floor was awfully cold and hard."

I shook my head in gratitude that, through it all, my Mom hadn't lost her sense of humor and I even teased in return, "Well, that's why we like for you to sleep in your bed, Mom!" Bless her; she gets it and chuckles before falling asleep.

The immediate crisis was past, but everyone knew that Mom could not continue like that. The caregivers and we couldn't either. So although I was expecting a call to address how we would deal with these new developments in Mom's condition, I was not prepared for the voice on the phone chirping a veritable birdsong of promise. "Well, we don't know why your Mom is suddenly losing strength, but I think I can work with her and bring her back to normal." I was speechless. It seriously occurred to me that the physical therapist calling with her assessment of how to keep Mom from falling had gotten her records mixed up and should have been singing that melody to someone else. Or had she evaluated the wrong resident at Mountainview?

The sunny tune continued, "She's pretty strong, and such a trooper. I even walked her around a while!"

A trooper? Oh yes, it appallingly dawned on me, she had seen Mom alright! And because I could suddenly picture my mother painfully dragging herself around in her ever-present attempt at polite cooperation, I flew into a rage. "Actually," I hissed, "we know exactly why she is getting weaker. My Mom is dying of a debilitating disease. Furthermore, there is absolutely nothing sudden about her decline. And the train for *normal* left the station years ago, and we're not on it."

My tirade over, there was silence until the voice, decidedly less cheery, ventured tentatively, "So, uhm, you don't *want* me to help her?"

I managed something marginally polite about needing to consult with my sister and hung up. Then I put my head onto my desk and wept. My God, does she really not understand how *much* I want her to help Mom?

But that help, Ute and I agreed when I called her at her office after regaining some composure, would not come by forcing, urging, or shaming Mom into doing what we all knew she could not do. Mom herself, we were certain, understood better than the rest of us that she would never walk again. Those were her legs and they had faithfully carried her all those years and untold miles. Now, Ute and I were certain, despite all of Mom's own effort and the help of professionals, she and her legs would not go farther. Above all, we agreed that it was not Mom's job to try harder to meet our needs, but our obligation to understand hers. It was the least we could do to be as helpful as possible.

From friends and professionals I had heard nightmarish stories about making end-of-life decisions when family members disagree on a course of action for their loved one. Nothing of the sort was the case with Ute and me. That situation made me realize again what a gift it was that the two of us were of one mind about what was best for Mom. Since our understanding of "best" did not involve cajoling her to participate more actively in our world, we solemnly agreed when Mountainview's director suggested that it might be time to involve Hospice in Mom's care plan.

The Hospice Care conference Curtis and I attended later that week was at once comforting and disturbing. Hospice staff began by assuring us that a person can, in fact, "graduate" from Hospice care should their condition improve. But the unspoken truth resonated in the room louder than those words: most people draw Hospice into the patient care plan because of a diagnosis, and the tacit agreement that the person is "actively" dying. We took the step well aware that Medicare rules require that a patient be certified as terminal (not expected to live more than six months) in order to qualify for federal reimbursement of Hospice services. We had entered a new stage in Mom's illness and knew it, but still a few points in the conversation did catch us off guard.

In his initial assessment of Mom's health and her family's relationship to her, the physician looked directly at Curtis and me. "Are you still able to have sensible conversations with your Mom?"

Without missing a beat we replied in unison, "Oh, yes, absolutely!" This was true. But we went silent just as quickly, looked at each other, and recognized to what degree we had bent the truth. "Well, if you know Mom and her history, her world still makes sense," I offered. "If you ignore that I am often her mother and sometimes her sister, and accept that her dad had visited her room earlier that day, then you can have a coherent conversation." "And," I continued, "if it doesn't matter that she sees Curtis as the six-year-old for whom she used to fix school lunches rather than the thirty-six-year-old man standing before her, then it all makes sense."

Since we did know those things, even spoke the German she now used almost exclusively, and messages conveyed in touch and laughter are universally understood anyway, sure, we could still have sensible communication with Mom! The doctor made some notes and smiled kindly. "Okay."

Next we needed to address decisions about Mom's overall treatment plan. Mom had a legal living will in place and an official "Do Not Resuscitate" order on file. But there are other killers, ones that don't lend themselves to the drastic, lifesaving response of resuscitation—or absence thereof. Shall we continue to administer the adult maintenance dose of aspirin Mom is taking daily to ward off strokes, for example? We didn't even know whether it was preventing them, let alone whether a stroke might not be a faster, kinder way to end Mom's suffering. Again, Curtis's and my eyes locked across the conference room table as that medication was eliminated from Mom's care plan. And what about treating any secondary conditions that might arise?

Whether brought on by aspiration or bacterial contamination, probably the greatest threat to a bed-bound individual's life is pneumonia. On the other hand, pneumonia has been known throughout time as "the old man's friend" for allowing the death of a body determined to hold on through pain and misery. Friend or foe, if, and more likely when, pneumonia strikes, it is important to have already decided whether to treat the cause. Although the role of Hospice care is to alleviate one's suffering while dying rather than to attempt to change the course of the disease, the distinction between palliative and curative care is not as clear as one might like. Our main goal was to keep Mom *comfortable*. Knowing that and repeating that mantra was easy. But there is nothing comfortable about not being able to breathe as one's lungs slowly grow too congested to take in vital air. One obvious way to relieve the stress of bacterial pneumonia is with antibiotics. Would we want that? Curtis and I took several sharp breaths before we shook our heads. "No, we do not want the pneumonia treated." "Mom," I restated, "would not want the pneumonia treated."

Thoughtfully, Curtis spoke up. "It would be different if she had a *life* to come back to after the pneumonia is cured."

The physician nodded. "Right. I don't hear you speaking *for* your Mom, I hear you stating what she can no longer express to us in words."

With that, our decisions went on record. The change in Mom's condition was highlighted in bright yellow on her paperwork, and Mom's caregivers were clearly made aware of her new status: "AND" (Allow Natural Death). Mom was now officially a dying Hospice patient. In fact, it had been true for quite some time, of course. But Curtis and I had spoken the words that openly declared it so. Having freed Mom from the need to pretend otherwise just to keep us comfortable, we left the conference greatly relieved.

I DON'T KNOW when the worry and sadness came for Curtis, but for me the hours at night, before exhaustion gave way to sleep, were the betrayers. Dark doubts took over my mind. Had we, not the disease, condemned Mom? Were we truly honoring *her* wish to die, or merely seeking to relieve our own inability to share her suffering?

Worse yet was that now *life* had no value beyond awaiting death. Normal life-events seemed to reverse their meaning. I was almost grateful when Mom was having a "bad" day. Seeing her unable to leave her bed, or show no interest in visitors, meals, or weather was convoluted confirmation that we had made the right decision. Mom would and could not regain a better quality of life.

On the other hand, Mom's good days were perversely excruciating. Like the Sunday in late May when I found Mom sitting in her wheelchair happily participating in activities. The game for the day was badminton. Made for the very young or very old, the paddles and birdie were of foam rubber that couldn't injure anyone regardless of who got hit where or how hard. Still the scene was a bit reminiscent of our delightful family weekends of fifty years earlier. Badminton and ping pong were the two games our family played enthusiastically and well. On many a rainy winter day, our huge hallway in Aumühle would be transformed into a gym with a regulation-size ping-pong table. With enough room on either end for the players and extra space along the sides, Dad would cheerfully call out advice about playing the feather-light ball tight and close to the net. Or better yet, slice it low and hard. With prac-tice one could land it just barely on the other side of the net to then reverse direction and spin out of the opponent's reach.

During spring and summer, we'd just as frequently pack

a picnic and the badminton set. Unlike in ping-pong, a successful badminton return calls for a broader underhanded swing,
giving the birdie more lift to launch it and carry it over the
net. My dad's admonition to play this game "high" so that the
birdie could easily clear the net before sailing down on the
other side became chanted wisdom in our family. Anytime an
insufficiently launched birdie got caught in the net, rather than
cruising over it, we would sing out in unison, *"Federball spielt
man HOCH"* (badminton is played *high*) before we all broke
into laughter.

Ute playing badminton "high"
ca. 1960 in Aumühle

I clearly revisited
those cheerful outings
of my childhood as I sat
next to Mom, wondering
whether for her, too, those
memories were behind
her pleased, open expres-
sion. Something about the
game at Mountainview
had caught the imagina-
tion of many in the Activities group, and the foam
rubber birdie sometimes
flew, but mostly crashed
energetically, across the
room. Occasionally a hit
would come directly at me
and I'd return it. But usually I retrieved the birdies dropping
around Mom's wheelchair and handed them to her for dis-
patch. Hand-eye coordination was sorely tested, but Mom was
not deterred. With fierce concentration she placed the birdie
on her racket, looked around, recited *"Federball spielt man
hoch,"* and gave it a mighty heave.

In what I've since come to hold as a sacred moment, Mom
and I looked at each other knowingly, connecting to a time
when Dad's guidance and the family's laughter were still the
mortar of our lives. It brought me immense joy to have held
that bond, however briefly, reaching across the years and

changes to support Mom in that simple pleasure. I wasn't sure how long Mom's memory would allow her to retain a sense of that enjoyment, but I got my answer when I left Mom in her bed after dinner. Like a thoroughly happy child, Mom waved good night and added contentedly, *"Na, das hat aber Spass gemacht!"*

"Yes, dear Mom," I echoed, "that *was* great fun." After gently closing the door, I sneaked away from Mountainview sobbing. Hunched over the steering wheel, I stubbornly and stupidly clung to the idea that perhaps Mom *would* graduate from Hospice care and we had not rushed her toward death after all. My mind muddled by Mom's enjoyable afternoon and my sight hindered by unbidden and unstoppable tears, I sat for a long time before driving home—even then through a damp haze.

My dreams of badminton, a whole family's survival and Mom's recovery were dashed soon enough. As if she wanted to relieve my confusion over the meaning of good days and bad, by the next day Mom had resumed her undeniable decline. Though there was some comfort in that the wheelchair Hospice had ordered for her did free Mom from having to walk again, its ever-present bulk in the room made the tasks of Mom's daily care and hygiene much more difficult. Getting her from bed to wheelchair to commode and then back to the wheelchair and to bed had become a real and frightening ordeal. I despised the degradation she had to endure for something as natural as emptying her bowels. To save her at least from having to do so with strangers, I timed my visits to be the one helping her. That way I was assured that we would both be rewarded with a warm embrace afterward. Following one particularly taxing excursion to the bathroom, I snuggled next to Mom in bed and said out loud how very much we loved her. I felt her embrace tightening around me in understanding before I went on to remind her that there was absolutely nothing she need be afraid of.

In response, Mom's grip on me loosened to a gentle pat. She didn't open her eyes, but continued to pat me reassuringly. With her spirit obviously much more ordered than either her body or my mind, a smile softened her face: "Oh, I'm not worried. I'm just *so* tired."

Beyond the Horizon:
June 12-19, 2006

"Care I for the limb, the thews, the stature, bulk and big assemblence of a man? Give me his spirit. "
–Shakespeare

JUST EXACTLY HOW tired Mom was of it all was brought home with unmistakable clarity only a couple of weeks later. On the Monday that would begin, to the day, the last week of her life, Mom had fallen out of bed again and been found on the floor by the morning caregivers. After the staff had hoisted Mom back to bed in what must have been another embarrassing torment for her, Mountainview's director called my office with the news. I listened with impatient alarm and cut her off mid-sentence to say that I was on my way to be with Mom. "Let's talk further when I get there."

Along the way, snippets of "one of the caregivers hurt her back trying to hold your Mom," and "we'll have to consider other solutions for her care" buzzed in my head like a swarm of angry bees. Everyone, most of all Mom, had tried with dignity and good spirit to accept and cope with the changes the disease had forced on her. We were all, it seemed to me, quickly running out of alternatives, and I couldn't imagine *what* other solutions there could be.

The usual fifteen-minute drive to Mountainview seemed endless, and I raced into the building fully aware that there was much to discuss. But my first concern remained for Mom. Not knowing how I would find her, or for that matter, what I would say to her, I was initially relieved to see that her door

167

stood wide open. I could walk right in. Then it struck me: the last vestige of her dignity, the privacy of a closed door to *her* room, had given way to the greater need for her to be watched. Damn it.

But if Mom took offense at that exposure she didn't show it. She was much too determined to express another emotion. Instead of her usual, vacant gaze, Mom's eyes were focused unflinchingly on the wall. She didn't even turn her head to look at me as I approached, and she continued to stare straight ahead when I sat on her bed and took her hand. "Oh Mom, does anything hurt? Do you feel better now that you're back in bed?" I stroked her hair and tugged at the sheets. "Would you like me to move this pillow to make your head more comfortable?" I couldn't stop fidgeting and babbling.

But Mom's steely silence and the stern resolve flashing in her eyes sent an unmistakable message of pure anger the more recognizable for its rarity. It was so unlike her. This was no time for platitudes. She was taking no chances that the disgust she felt with her situation might be mitigated as she hissed, "*Wenn Einen da drei Leute hochwraggeln müssen ist es aber wirklich genug!*" (When it takes three people to wrestle you up off the floor, then it truly *is* enough!)

It wasn't embarrassment or lack of courage Mom was feeling. A roiling fury caused her to make and voice her decision that life under those circumstances was no longer worth living. The strength of her declaration warned me not to argue, even if I could have thought of something reasonable with which to counter her feelings. As it was, I didn't even want to try. Instead of patronizing her with Pablum, I swallowed my impotence and accepted her self-knowledge and determination by burrowing next to her in bed. We held each other in silence. Mom slept calmly, utterly at ease now that her brain had finally let her express what she so urgently wanted us to know. I lay gratefully considering the message, and held it and Mom as I would cradle a fledgling fallen from its nest that I could save only by letting it quietly die.

I stayed snuggled next to Mom a long time and didn't seek out Mountainview's director to discuss that ever-present "what now" until much later. Once Julie and I did meet, she used equal measures of empathy and pragmatism as we searched for creative solutions for keeping Mom safe in "her" room for the rest of her life while protecting the staff from physical injury. As an assisted living facility, Mountainview is prohibited by federal law from using full hospital beds with railings in the residents' rooms. Given that rule, I doubted we could find ways for keeping Mom from falling out of bed. Julie was already a step ahead. "Have you seen those pregnancy pillows?" she ventured. She described huge, cushiony mounds that billow up on either side of the expectant mother. When she's lying down, they connect in place with a Velcro strip underneath her back to offer soft but firm support when weight and lack of coordination threaten to tip her onto her side—or out of bed altogether. "I already bought a couple and I think they'll help your Mom feel secure and keep her from rolling too far."

With the image of Mom's crystal-clear response to her acute distress still stinging, I wasn't in the mood yet to consider steps that would only prolong Mom's struggle. Still, I had to agree that such pillows might work. As Julie said, they would at least make Mom feel more secure.

Next, Julie mentioned that a family had left Mountainview a bed—legally permissible because it was not the official hospital model—that would raise Mom's chest or feet and consequently make it much easier for her to sit up. Would I agree to moving Mom from her own bed into that one, rearranging her room a bit, and thereby allowing her to become completely bed-bound?

Why not, I thought. "Sure." The open door to Mom's room hadn't left her much of her precious privacy. We might as well trade in her comfy-cozy bed.

Finally, after a moment of hesitation, Julie suggested another session with a physical therapist, this time someone from Hospice. The proverbial red flag in front of the bull, I snapped at the bait. "We've tried that, and I'm not putting Mom through it again."

Refusing to accept the position of adversary, Julie quickly explained, "No, not for Ilse to do things differently! But for someone to teach my staff how to transfer and support her better without hurting themselves."

I muttered an apology as I was again reminded that Mountainview really was on our side. And that Julie, in particular, was absolutely determined not to let Mom's disease force her from the room, people, and surroundings that had been her home for two and a half years. "Oh, right, I guess that'll be best."

The approach and demeanor of the Hospice physical therapist could not have been more appropriate, and different, from our earlier experience. She spent several hours on Tuesday morning with Mom, the staff, and me. Her sensitivity to Mom and expertise at her trade were exceptional. While I was still not hopeful, I began to believe that Mom might get through this next stage of her life's end with some dignity. Mom herself participated in the exercises and was clearly worn out by them. It was her body we were rearranging and jostling about, but she tolerated the exercises with such obvious mental distance from the activity that we might as well have been worrying about someone else's future. Mom, my Mom, was not involved.

She was calmly ensconced amid a soft mountain of pillows holding her in place, and was not, whether for meals or bathroom visits, encouraged to leave her overstuffed nest. Whatever the question—was she hungry or thirsty, would she like to watch TV, was she too hot amid all those covers—her response was a benign smile. "No, thank you. I'm always very *comfortable* in *my* bed."

Mom's peace of mind—her physical condition being almost irrelevant to her compared to her mental well-being at being "comfortable in *my* bed"—also brought us relief. There are schools of thought in the field of Memory Care advocating that once an assisted living facility can no longer meet a certain standard of care for the physical needs of a dementia patient, it may be time to move that individual into skilled nursing care. Each type of institution is designed and staffed to meet different needs of the ill or aging. And in the best of all possible worlds, matching the appropriate care with the specific, changing needs of the fragile elderly population no doubt represents the highest ideal worth striving for.

Unfortunately, we felt that Mom's dementia did not allow us to choose between *bests*. Instead we felt forced to make choices between respecting Mom's personal preferences and desires, her psychological needs, and most proficiently addressing her physical decline. We opted for respecting her expressed wishes of remaining peacefully in place in favor of moving her to another facility, with the accompanying distress of unfamiliar routines and faces. That was a personal choice made by our family in consideration of what we believed to be true about our Mom's lifelong convictions. And it may have come at the expense of some of her physical needs being somewhat less ably handled by assisted living caregivers or family members than they would have been in a nursing home. But for us, honoring our Mom's one desire to remain "comfortable" throughout her illness was paramount. And for making that decision possible for us, we are ever grateful to the director and staff at Mountainview. They provided us with both excellent physical care for Mom and the flexibility that allowed us, within the rules of law, to also meet Mom's psychological and emotional needs. Institutional ideals are rarely flexible enough to be tempered by human reality and we consider ourselves fortunate to have come upon one that was so.

Because looking back on those last days, it is not exaggerating to say that Mom's greatest comfort was that she was safely in bed and finally allowed to let go of life on her own terms. Her physical competence declined more rapidly than at any other time throughout her disease. But her mind seemed more coherent and determined than we'd seen it in years. I will never know where she found the strength and lucidity to orchestrate that last week of her life. But I know now that Mom had a plan, and armed with a plan she had always been formidable. Now more than ever, she would not be deterred.

By Thursday, things were going so smoothly that Paul and I had a long afternoon visit with Mom. Based on how we felt Mom was doing, we would make a final decision about whether I should attend a long-planned Wehr family reunion in Pittsburgh over the weekend. We arrived right after lunch and, initially, the sight of Mom so thoroughly in bed set Paul back a bit. But that was nothing compared to our surprise at hearing Mom ask repeatedly how Paul's leg was doing. Had she really grasped, and was she now actually remembering his recent months in a cast with a broken ankle? Anyway, she certainly knew something had been wrong with his legs as she said that her legs didn't hurt today either. By way of explanation she added that ever-soothing, "I'm always so comfortable in *my* bed."

When we moved Mom into Mountainview, I'd promised myself that I would do everything I could to stem the tide of loneliness I saw in so many eyes there. Removed from their interaction with "normal" life and robbed of their ability to recognize family, friends, and even themselves, I could only imagine how alone many of the residents must have felt.

One reliable way for me to bridge that isolation for Mom was to regularly apply lotion to her hands, arms, legs, and feet. It was necessary. In Colorado the high, dry air draws moisture from all manner of life, including human skin, producing dehydration. Besides, it gave us a good excuse to touch, regularly affirming our tactile bond. It made sense that thoroughly lotioning Mom became our treasured ritual and healthy habit. As Mom's disease advanced, I couldn't always tell whether she still wished to be touched as much as I longed to feel her warmth. Often, I got my answer. After we finished and Mom was nestled "comfy-cozy" under her covers, she'd close her eyes and sigh, "That feels so good. My Mum did that for me yesterday."

So when I snuggled up next to Mom to lotion her on that Thursday, and Paul responded to our conspiratorial intimacy by teasing us as he had for years, Mom's mind was so clear that she even played along. She remembered her part of the script! Whenever she and I headed off on one of our outings, Paul would joke, finger wagging in mock warning, "Now, don't you two girls get into trouble!"

Listening to Paul feeding her the line, Mom kept her eyes closed. But a familiar softness lit her face. With more of a grin than a smile, her response was as flirtatious as she had ever allowed herself to get. "Sure," she would reassure Paul

sweetly, "we'll be good." A self-possessed seventeen-year-old with an agenda couldn't have sounded more compliant. But the other half of the message was implicit in Mom's demeanor. "But if we decided to pull one over on you, you'd never know about it!" We all chuckled and nodded our heads in relief, our complicity proof that, at least for that moment, the three of us were in the same place and time.

No question, Mom's spirit and body were calmer than we'd found them in a long time. That made for a good visit. An exceptional one really, and in that recognition I agreed with everyone that it was not only reasonable, but probably important on other levels of our lives too, that I join Paul on the brief trip to Pittsburgh. It was the unanimous feeling that we should get away and relax. I was reassured by the promise of Hospice and Mountainview caregivers to get Mom through my absence with extra attention and love. I would also keep my cell phone handy.

ON FRIDAY JUNE 16, Paul and I took the 4:30 a.m. bus to Denver International Airport. Had we driven, our car would probably have taken the exit for Mountainview by force of habit. As it was, I watched the turn-off pass by with mixed emotions. Departures, even for happy occasions, had always forced me to acknowledge that some beloved place or person would not be accessible to me for a while. Leaving Mom had been difficult even when we'd had our good night hug and would be separated only until the next day, so heading out of town for three days was hard. But with memories of yesterday's visit, I tried to relax and look forward to the weekend as I boarded my flight.

Paul, who would be going on to Maine rather than returning to Colorado, took a different flight. We were to meet at the baggage carousel in Pittsburgh. But airline travel being what it is we also knew that we could be in touch by cell phone about altered plans or schedules. We reject the multi-tasking lifestyle of people with their phones glued to their ears while doing other things that we believe should be receiving their full attention. Still, a mobile phone would enable us to reach each other and other family members who would also be traveling great distances.

I didn't object to turning my phone off during the flight but switched it on immediately upon deplaning in Pittsburgh. I was eager to reconnect with Paul and learn whether, like mine, his flight had gone smoothly and arrived on time. So when the phone beeped urgently as I fired it up, I was excited. Great, everyone's already here! Just need to figure out where to meet the hotel shuttle, shower, change, and .... I was still spinning mental images of our reunion when the voice on the phone sent my spirits plummeting. "Chris, this is Susan at Mountainview. I don't want to worry you, but your Mom isn't breathing well. Please call me when you get this. I know how close you two are, and if I were you, I'd come home." Wham. A head-on with a bus could not have thrown me a stiffer blow.

I must have been getting some air, but my chest felt like an elephant was sitting on it and my heart was pounding in my throat, when I saw Paul walking down the concourse toward me. I don't think I even said hello before launching into my pain at not being with Mom when she needed me most. Protective of me, Paul's rational side took over as he wrapped his arms around me and said, "There's nothing you can do." Maybe because I knew how true that was, and that truth was the last thing I wanted to hear, I became angry and turned my frustration on him. "It's not about doing; it's about *being* there!"

Rebuffed, Paul went silent as I dialed the Mountainview number to learn what was going on. Susan, the nurse on duty, calmly told me that sometime during the morning Mom's breathing had become shallow and rapid. She didn't appear to be in pain, but was gasping at a rate of almost forty breaths per minute, and Susan had summoned the Hospice nurse to look in on Mom. She was on her way to do just that and would be there to give Mom morphine if she became restless.

We ended the conversation agreeing that I would find out when and how I could get back to Colorado. Once I knew about flight options, I'd call to talk with the Hospice nurse. With her assessment I could reevaluate the urgency of my return. Hearing only my side of that conversation, Paul's eyes were questioning and worried. But he soon knew, too, that if only to preserve my own sanity, I had to return to Colorado as quickly as possible. Still, there were many decisions, calls, and plans to be made; and we agreed to get to our hotel, update the family, and sort out further details somewhere quiet.

The extended Wehr and Stone families were already gathered in the hotel lobby awaiting their rides to the evening festivities when we arrived and explained the situation; my visit would be brief, at most. Their embraces were comforting and their response was uniform, "Of course, you must go back."

In our room, I collapsed on the bed, gulped several glasses of water with aspirin to combat my raging headache, and started dialing. I first called the airline. The agent, sensitive to my stressful situation, seemed to work furiously. But after almost thirty minutes of holding and listening to "Rhapsody in Blue," my cell phone bleated a warning before the "lost call" message flashed on the screen. I was ready to throw it against the wall when it occurred to me that at least this once I might actually use all the minutes for which I paid every month. Absurdly satisfied, I decided to call Mountainview before dialing back into the airline's reservations phone bank. I wanted to know whether the Hospice nurse had arrived, whether she could provide more information to help unscramble my emotions.

She had and she could. Her calm voice and thoughtful

presence next to Mom did much to reduce my sense of help-lessness; our conversation made the next fifteen hours bearable for me. Karen had given Mom a small dose of morphine to ease her breathing and agreed with Susan that I should return as quickly as possible. However, she was equally clear that she did not think Mom would suffer unduly through a night without me. While making no predictions, she said that from her experience with this final stage, she would not expect Mom to die in the next twelve hours.

Then came the diagnosis. "And you don't want us to treat the pneumonia—right?"

Hearing that pneumonia was the cause of that sudden change in Mom's condition stated so matter-of-factly caught me unprepared. The thought "they could treat it" flitted across my mind like a migrating bird off its route before I remembered Curtis's wise statement "...*if* she had a life to come back to" to myself. "No, we don't want the pneumonia treated," I heard a voice say that may or may not have been mine. Then I added defensively, "That's what Mom's directive already states."

Karen quickly responded that yes, she knew that, but had to ask. Families occasionally change their minds at this stage; and with all our earlier certainty dissolving into heartache, at that moment I wasn't sure either whether pneumonia was friend or foe. But I said nothing more.

Karen next asked if I wanted to talk to Mom. Oh yes, yes please! Mom can talk? Well, to say Mom and I then *talked* together is a stretch. But our halting and labored communication, even over the phone, helped me feel connected and provided the salve I needed. "Mom, I'm here; how are you?" Her breath coming in rapid, rasping gulps, she muttered a question that was the only answer I needed, "Chrissie?" She recognized my voice! "Yes, dear Mom. The nurse gave you some medication to make it easier for you to breathe."

"Okay."

"Mom, all you need to do is sleep and I'll be with you tomorrow morning—okay?"

It seemed to take all she had to give, but three words confirmed that Mom still thought both she and I were on the right course. "*Das ist gut.*" (That's good.)

With Mom approving my plan, I listened calmly as Karen returned to say that the morphine was starting to work; Mom would be breathing and resting more comfortably. Karen urged that I, too, should try to get some sleep for that trip home.

Good advice, to be sure, but also much easier said than done. I was reassured that Mom would hang on so as not to struggle alone through these last days of our journey together. But hearing Mom on the phone also left me acutely aware of how terribly far I was from where I wanted to be. There was only one more flight out of Pittsburgh that night—to Dallas. Given no delays, I might barely catch a plane there that would get me to Denver around seven the next morning. The other option was a direct flight leaving Pittsburgh very early Saturday putting me by Mom's side late the same morning. We had been up since 2:30 a.m. and sensing what lay ahead, Paul supported Karen's suggestion. "Join the family for some dinner, Chrissie. We'll get a few hours of rest and I'll take you back to the airport early." With the comfort of having heard Mom's voice, I agreed. Then I would take on what we knew would be Mom's deathwatch.

An hour later I was booked on that early Saturday flight returning me, with luck, to Mom before lunch. Feeling more like a lifetime, it would have been just over a day since I'd left her! More phone calls followed. Upon hearing my description of Mom's condition, Ute immediately explored ways to get to Colorado from Oregon. I reached Curtis who was driving to a volleyball tournament. He would be a four-hour mountain drive from Boulder, where he and his partner were playing in an event that could provide badly needed income for the summer. "Should I come back, Mom?"

My response was immediate and the one I honestly felt would have come from his beloved Omi. "No, Hon, not unless you think you want to. Ute and I will be there. Omi would want you to earn a paycheck and not let your partner down. Let's just talk when you can and we'll see you after the tournament."

I reached my friend Jennifer to arrange a ride from the

airport in Denver. She would be glad to meet me there. Ute called to say she had confirmed the last seat on the only flight out of the airport nearest to her isolated coastal home the next morning and would see me at the Boulder bus terminal late afternoon tomorrow. Lastly, I called Mountainview again to hear that Mom was asleep, resting. One of the caregivers had offered to stay by her side throughout the night, and as final reassurance, Susan reminded me that everyone had my cell phone number. They would report any change in Mom's condition immediately. It didn't bear mentioning that if things were to turn critical earlier than expected, they could call me, but there would be absolutely no way for me to get there faster.

I did relax a little around the food and festivities of that fiftieth wedding anniversary reunion. It was a genuine celebration of life; and Mom, the party planner extraordinaire, would have approved. I managed a few hours of sleep before Paul and I sat embracing in the shuttle-bus to the Pittsburgh airport. The plane was due to depart on time—good news. For if neither of us liked that rushed departure for our separate responsibilities for the summer, Paul and I knew that each of us would be doing exactly what our lives called for at that time. We held each other in deep love respecting that knowledge, and I headed into the still mostly empty concourse of the airport alone. My overnight bag slung over my shoulder, check-in was a breeze and my next stop was at a McDonald's. I eagerly sucked on a cup of coffee as I repeatedly checked the information monitors. Apparently, the weather looked good at both ends of the flight; everything should go according to schedule. Given the early hour, especially in Colorado, I did not call Mountainview until I was ready to board the plane.

"Your mom's doing fine. She slept quietly all night and is still sleeping."

Fine? It's amazing how the meaning of a word changes with the circumstances. It's all relative. But yes, settled into my window seat watching the plane bank to the west, I had to admit that now I, too, was fine.

I usually get a little queasy when something that, by gosh and by golly (and a little luck thrown in), just happens to work out as planned and is subsequently burdened with the heady declaration that, "it must have been *meant* to be." I get downright nauseous when the opposite is presumed; when something well-planned and hoped for falls victim to death and disaster and is then simplistically assumed to have been doomed from the start. My sense of predestination isn't nearly well developed enough to stomach such assertions. I'm unable to abide either the lack of control or the desperate hopelessness that attributing events to fate implies. But on that early morning flight west, with eastern Colorado already browned by an unusually hot May sun far below me—while my eyes scanned the horizon for any sign of something resembling the "Switzerland of America" for which Mom so earnestly searched more than forty years earlier—I was certain that, whatever lay ahead, I would make it to Mom's side to be with her as she died.

MAYBE IT *WAS* "meant to be," I wondered sheepishly as I stepped into Mom's room and gently leaned across her laboring chest to kiss her cheek. If she noticed my presence she gave no sign, but I didn't care. All I wanted was to be able to see her, hold her hands, and be there in case she woke up again, ever. I couldn't stop looking at Mom, and I was totally at ease, not so much with the dreadful situation but with the peace from my conviction that both Mom and I were precisely where we needed and wanted to be.

Having watched her own mother die of breast cancer, Jen understood what our family would be going through and knew I wouldn't be leaving Mom's room soon. Since it was nearly lunchtime when she picked me up at the airport, then dropping me off at Mom's, she offered to buy a favorite salad for us before meeting me back at Mountainview. I was happy for her company as we distractedly picked at our meals and talked freely—in a whisper. Although we wouldn't have disturbed Mom's heavy sleep, and we'd made no conscious decision to be quiet, our shared sense of sacred space seemed to call for hushed voices.

Then there was a knock at the door. One of the Mountainview caregivers came in carrying a plate heaped high with a hot dog, coleslaw, baked beans, and a brownie. I suddenly remembered that it was the annual Mountainview Father's Day BBQ, and it crossed my mind how kind it was of the staff to bring us some food. Before I could say, "Thank you so much, but my friend brought some salads," the young woman set the plate on the nightstand next to Mom's closed, absent face.

"Here is some lunch for Ilse."

Dumbfounded, Jen and I stared at each other. We were somewhat confused but decided to settle on humor and exchanged amused glances instead of bursting out, "For crying out loud, Mom can't breathe! Do you really expect she'll be munching on a hot dog?" Better to laugh at the absurdity than to get angry. No harm was intended.

But honestly, this was a Memory Care Assisted Living facility; Mom had been in Hospice Care for six weeks, bedridden for most of those, and was now slipping, with those last gasping breaths, into her final morphine-induced rest. Yet even in this place of trained caregivers, the dying process is so removed from our concept of life that it is less awkward to offer her a lunch plate as she was dying than to face the fact that she would never eat again. "Thanks, but I don't think she'll be eating that" was all I could muster before the caregiver, eyes downcast, shuffled off.

Jen sat with us into the afternoon before offering to pick up Ute so I wouldn't have to leave Mom. When it was time for her to do so, she leaned forward and tenderly kissed Mom on the cheek. She folded Mom's hands in hers, took a long breath, and with tears gathering said, "Sleep well, dear Ilse." Just that. Not something idiotic like, "I hope you feel better," or "See you tomorrow." Rather, Jen found the words for the most appropriate wish for a calm passage. Sleep well. The sensitivity she learned came at a hard price, the loss of her own mother. But I will remain forever grateful that Mom and I were the beneficiaries of her compassionate, understanding friendship.

Once Mom and I were alone in her room, her breathing dominated our togetherness. The steady, rhythmic rise and fall of her chest demanded all of my attention as, with each short exhalation, I held my own breath until Mom's lungs slowly and heavily expanded to take in the next burdened gulp of air. I wasn't scared or worried, just narrowly focused on the process, unable to decide whether I was wishing for that next life-preserving breath for her or waiting for her body to simply and finally go calm.

Tired and wanting to be close, I leaned into Mom's bed from my chair and rested my head on her pillow. For some reason I didn't close my eyes, though, and had them fixed on Mom when she opened hers. Wide, bright, beautifully brown, they momentarily lit her whole expression in smiling recognition and, with all the inflection of joyous, affectionate wonder, Mom clearly spoke the last thing she would ever say to me. "Oh, hi Chrissie!" "Oh, hi my dear Mom," I smiled back as I kissed and embraced her. She did not hold me in return, her heavy lids closed again, and the moment was gone. But all that mattered was that the moment had occurred.

I have no idea how long I lay hunched over Mom's shoulder. It couldn't have been an hour. But it was long enough to give me a fierce crick in my neck by the time I was released from my awkward position by a tentative knock on the door. When Ute's face appeared I was overjoyed. She didn't say anything at first, just glanced at Mom, then me, and solemnly nodded her head. It was right and good that we were here, together, now. After greeting Mom with a hug that received no noticeable response, Ute and I held each other tightly. I was never so happy and thankful to see my sister.

It wasn't long before Susan, still on duty, came into the room to tell us she was going home for the night. Arrangements had to be made for administering the morphine. Ute and I weren't leaving, so we agreed to do whatever was required. A precise .25 mg. had to be sucked into the eyedropper and placed under Mom's tongue every four hours. Since we were dealing with a controlled substance, Susan stressed the importance of recording and accounting for every drop. As always, more concerned with Mom's comfort than anything else, we would do both tasks without question. Apparently Mom never felt a thing. She didn't even need to swallow as the viscous liquid was almost instantly absorbed into her mucous membranes to take effect.

As darkness fell and the reality of the physical and emotional miles we'd traveled that day could no longer be denied, we decided we had better do something about our own sleeping arrangements. Ute was content to scoot into a sleeping bag on the floor by Mom's feet, and I put two chairs together to fashion something to stretch out on right next to Mom. We were dog-tired, but rest was nevertheless elusive and Ute and I talked late into the night. Family memories, loves and losses, and occasional laughter were interspersed with comments on Mom's breathing and our relief that she seemed comfortable.

After giving the midnight dose of morphine, Ute and I fell into an uneasy sleep—at least until Mom got restless. We were still several hours from the next allowable relief dose for Mom when her hands started tearing at her bedding and clothes. I didn't want to physically restrain her, so I crawled into bed with her and stroked and held her agitated arms. She'd drop off again for a moment, before the edgy movements would start again. Sometimes she'd mutter something I couldn't understand. But my response was always the same: "It's okay dear Mom; we're all here, there's nothing to worry about."

Only once did she say something comprehensible, and, with Ute finally asleep on the floor, it was accurate as well. *"Da schnarcht jemand."* (Somebody is snoring).

To me her observation seemed like a comfortable awareness that she was not alone, and I couldn't help but grin in the otherwise bitter darkness.

"Yes Mom, Ute is sleeping here with us. Isn't that nice?"

In response I got only Mom's empty eyes searching into space and her wandering hands grasping at her blankets, legs, and belly.

The sun took its own sweet time appearing in the eastern sky, and the hours crept by slowly. Long before daylight softened the room, Ute stirred stiffly on the floor. "Darn firm mattress!" she chuckled and her laughter broke through my loneliness like a song. She came over and held me. Her query, "You didn't get much rest, did you," was more a statement, and within minutes she was in the Mountainview kitchen fixing coffee and toast for us.

At six, I finally called Hospice to express our concern at Mom's troubled night. The nurse said she'd be right over, and she did her best to restore my courage over the phone. She explained that Mom's frantic searching movements last night are quite common in the very final stages of life. Evidence suggests that this behavior is involuntary and, unconscious for Mom, was likely not nearly as stressful for her as it had been for me. But my mind was not easy. Something about Mom's medication had to be changed. This was not the comfortable passing we had promised we'd assure for Mom.

By the time Beth arrived, Ute and I had further bolstered our resolve and wasted no time. "Regardless of who suffered how much," I began firmly, "last night was unacceptable as palliative care management."

"There *are* definitely other medications available to us," Beth countered patiently. "We just don't want to give your Mom too much."

"What," I burst out, "is *too much* at this point?"

"Well," her reply was weighed and deliberate, "your Mom's breathing would slow down even further and she'd be very hard to rouse."

I wish I could blame my cross response on my lack of sleep. The truth was I was offended at being treated like a child who wasn't aware of what lay ahead. And I said so. "Pretty soon," I said angrily, "Mom is going to be impossible to rouse, and we are determined to keep our promise to help her get to her final rest comfortably. Far from being "too much," the medication so far has been woefully inadequate to accomplish that. And that needs to change, now."

"Of course, Chris," Beth's tone was now addressing an adult. "I just had to hear you say that you are aware of the consequences."

The "consequence" of doubling the amount of morphine,

still not half of the allowable dosage, and adding something to settle Mom's nervous system, was peaceful rest for her. She didn't notice the intrusion of caregivers changing her panties and sheets, or washing and checking her body for bedsores any more than she noticed the loving visitors who appeared. As far as we could tell, she never heard our reading her favorite German children's book to her or the music in the background. Throughout the day Mom's expression changed visibly into that of someone no longer present. Her eye sockets and cheek bones protruded, her limbs hung at clumsy angles unless we moved and supported them, and her mouth, though slightly open with the rasping flow of air, seemed to lose more life than it gained with each breath. No one brought lunch for Mom, but several caregivers came in to say goodbye. She had finally convinced everyone that she had to leave, and, accepting her plan, we were letting her go.

Ute and I each took a short break from our vigil. I went home to shower and change clothes, and although I noticed a beautiful June sky, I forgot that it was Father's Day and didn't relax again until I was back in Mom's room. Mike and his family came down from Fort Collins to take Ute out for a quick lunch, but we all knew why we were here together, and no one was totally at ease until we were at Mom's side. Despite the deep sadness around Mom's final labor and our impending loss, there was nowhere else Ute and I wanted to be.

Although the type of medication and the dosage had been changed, Mom remained on the "every four hours" morphine schedule. That kept her calm and was no problem for us to maintain throughout the day. However, following the ten p.m. dose, Ute and I decided we had better set an alarm if we were not to miss the two a.m. dose. We were exhausted and even with our uncomfortably rigged sleeping arrangements feared we might not wake up at the proper time. I didn't. Thankfully, though the alarm for some reason did not go off, Ute did wake up and gently roused me. "Chris, it's two. I think Mom needs her next round of meds."

Mom didn't stir as I dripped the morphine under her tongue, and Ute and I only talked for a little while. What a good thing there were two of us! But why hadn't the damned alarm gone off?

We did not mention that the sound of Mom's breathing had become a rattle. After each exhalation, there was a distinct gurgling in her throat, bubbles of mucous from her chest obstructing the body's next urge to inhale. We both heard it and knew what it meant, but listened in dark silence rather than disturb the sanctity of the work with chatter. We also didn't touch the alarm clock. It obviously wasn't reliable and we were very sure that if we slept again at all, we'd wake long before the six a.m. dose was due.

We were both dozing when the alarm went off. It had apparently decided that 2:45 a.m. was precisely the right moment for us to be jarred awake. I cursed the intrusion muttering something like, "What the hell..." as Ute scrambled for the "off" button. Not knowing what had made it ring in the first place—it was nowhere near the two o'clock to which the alarm-hand still pointed—we exchanged puzzled looks. "Weird."

Too tired to worry about a cranky clock, we settled back into our Spartan beds. Within seconds, and in unison, we were sitting bolt upright again. This time Ute turned the light on and we held each other's eyes, reverently absorbing the silence. Mom was no longer breathing. We got up together and each walked to one side of the bed to hold Mom's hands. Her eyes remained closed, her face unchanged. After a lifetime of one automatic inhalation for every exhalation, she finally failed to take that next breath.

For several seconds, or was it minutes, Mom's chest would heave spastically in an occasional involuntary, meaningless gasp, but before three o'clock on Monday morning, June 19, there was only silence in Mom's room at Mountainview. Ute and I just sat. We held Mom and each other. We thought, cried, nodded and smiled, but couldn't bring ourselves to break the stillness.

One of Mom's favorite liturgical settings had been the "Tenebrae Service of Shadows and Sorrows" traditionally used for the Lutheran Good Friday Worship. The evening of somber remembrance is centered on the "Seven Last Words of Christ."

I don't know whether Ute knew that; but when she broke our silence with the last words attributed to Jesus on the cross, "It is finished," it was the most beautiful tribute to our Mom and our vigil I could have imagined.

"*Es ist vollbracht.*" To Ute's and my ears, our native tongue often still seems more precise than its English linguistic cousin and that was particularly true at that moment. The English translation has Jesus giving himself over to death leaving this world with, "It is finished." But Mom's life and our journey together had not only been finished. Stated with good German precision, "*Es ist vollbracht;*" they had been fulfilled.

Epilogue: December 2007

*"What interests me most is to retain impressions, rather than
just the facts, of this unimaginable experience. "*
–Bertrand Piccard

MUCH OF WHAT gets planned, packed, and portaged for a
great expedition is essential and gets fully used up along the
way. Yet again as much seems to need sorting, putting away,
and restocking when the trip is over. But for the journey my
Mom and I took, even while staying in place, what needed orga-
nizing at the end was a great deal more than dirty laundry,
leftover food, and undeveloped film.

Once Ute and I had had
our private time of saying
good-bye to Mom that day,
we finally called Hospice
about four a.m. As soon as
Mom's death was official-
ly certified, the next call
was to the mortuary. The
undertakers asked several
times whether we wanted to
see Mom again before they
removed her body. No. Ute

"Well done, good and faithful servant"
Matthew 25:21

and I were happy to walk in the garden while they moved Mom's
body from the room, content in knowing that a rich and loving
life had been nobly fulfilled. I would have disagreements with
our Creator about the rules of the game of life, and what is more
important, about how and why our time here on Earth must
end. But since those rules are non-negotiable, we were comfortable knowing Mom had played her game exceptionally well.

187

Curtis, Mike, and his wife Angela worked furiously to empty Mom's room at Mountainview while Ute and I braced for the necessary discussions of the burial and memorial service arrangements. There were numerous phone calls to be made, and for no apparent reason, I talked my way through most of them just fine, while during a few I fell apart before finishing the first sentence, "Mom died this morning...."

But on the whole, the day went remarkably smoothly. I only had one real mental hiccup. After unloading Mom's last possessions into our garage, all of us decided that we needed a break and decided to go out for lunch. Once everyone had piled into the car, I was struck by the panic of having forgotten to do something important. I actually got out of the car and headed for our house to make a phone call. We had forgotten Mom! Her whole beloved family was assembled and going to lunch, and my only natural response to such an occasion was to phone Mom and let her know we were on our way to pick her up to join us! But I didn't make it to the house. The car door slamming shut behind me jolted me back to reality, and even though I noticed that everyone in the car exchanged bewildered glances, I kept the reason for that quick exit to myself. I quietly slid back behind the wheel and we headed for our favorite restaurant.

The truth was that while Mom's death signaled the final, permanent loss, her disease had long ago robbed us of the opportunity to share such a gathering. At that moment, and frequently since at that visceral ache of missing her, I find deep comfort in knowing that Mom is at rest. It is infinitely easier for me to walk away from her grave, after having shared my sandwich on a particularly beautiful sunny day with her at the cemetery, than it ever was to leave her at Mountainview, confused and alone.

And while she is resting in her well-deserved peace, our lives continue—without her presence, but never without her love and guidance. Ute and I talk occasionally of that strange alarm call on the morning of Mom's death. Neither of us is particularly inclined toward the supernatural, and if both of us hadn't been there, we'd probably be just as happy to forget exactly how it happened that we were awakened at the precise moment Mom took her last breath. And sometimes we wonder, "Come on, what *did* make the alarm go off then?" According to the clock's face and hands, the alarm did not ring at its appointed time; but as far as Mom's life was concerned, it could not have been more correct in waking us. Knowing my penchant for sound sleep, and we never having been as punctual as Mom, could she not have had one more gift for us—a plan to assure that her daughters would be awake the instant they most wanted to be so? And a lasting gift it was.

Curtis is in his second year of elementary school teaching and has found a free and mature voice speaking for children, diversity, and justice. I don't wonder where he got that! Paul and I left our Maine *Paradise* long enough last summer to explore beautiful Newfoundland and Labrador in our faithful VW camper. We're already planning more trips to places we are eager to share as a couple.

I have retired from the University, have run my first marathon (and am training for another), and have a new pair of "stinky barn-pants." Just as were the jeans Mom had to relegate to the cellar in Aumühle after returning from our vacations on the farm, these are also too smelly for wearing in public—but perfect for my horse-handling volunteer work at the outstanding "Colorado Therapeutic Riding Center." I think Mom would be pleased!

Now I'm eager to learn what else lies ahead. My life changed after Mom's death; it will never be the same. Sometimes it feels much heavier for the emptiness her absence has brought. At other times it feels decidedly easier and lighter than it has in a long while. I have been a daughter my whole life—longer than anything else in my fifty-seven years. I've been a mother well over half of those years, and a lover and wife for decades now. What else will define my identity as a whole woman shall be revealed.

But there will always be my deep gratitude for the privilege of traveling with my beloved Mom as we both sought, and found, our mothers.

Boulder, Colorado
April, 2008

Nourishment for Your Journey:

Chapter Discussion Questions

Notes for Your Own Provisions: <u>Introduction</u>

*What images will help you frame the story
of your care-giving journey?*

Notes for Your Own Provisions: <u>Home Base</u>

How do your reflections on your childhood home help or hinder your care-giving role?

Notes for Your Own Provisions: <u>A Sea Change</u>

Do you remember your first fear-filled suspicions about the state of your loved one's health?

Notes for Your Own Provisions: <u>Approaching Denial</u>

Was there an incident, or diagnosis, beyond denial that made you somehow aware that your life would change forever?

Notes for Your Own Provisions: <u>In Uncharted Waters</u>

Can you recall the first time your loved one behaved in a way that made no sense to you or could not be explained away?

Notes for Your Own Provisions: <u>New Landscapes</u>

Were you ever tempted to ask your loved one
whether they weren't feeling like themselves because
you didn't recognize them?

Notes for Your Own Provisions: <u>A Wrong Turn</u>

How do you handle situations in which your loved one acts on things you do not see or experience?

Notes for Your Own Provisions: <u>Off the Path</u>

*In what ways does your loved one's forgetting or dementia
separate him/her from your world?*

Notes for Your Own Provisions: <u>Lost</u>

Do you allow yourself to ask for help?

Notes for Your Own Provisions: <u>Making Camp</u>

*From whom and under what circumstances do you
find solutions?*

Notes for Your Own Provisions: <u>Unsettled Territory</u>

*What part of your care-giving role makes you feel
insufficient or imperfect?*

Notes for Your Own Provisions: <u>Longing for Home</u>

*How do you deal with the loss of your relationship
when your loved one doesn't recognize you?*

Notes for Your Own Provisions: <u>Fading into the Night</u>

*What do people say to you that indicates they have no idea
what you're going through and feeling?*

Notes for Your Own Provisions: <u>End of the Rainbow</u>

Have you had an opportunity to learn about
your loved one's "end-of-life" choices, or do you have any
personal decisions and wishes for him or her?

Notes for Your Own Provisions: <u>Beyond the Horizon</u>

*Have you thought about what it might feel like
when your loved one passes away?*

Notes for Your Own Provisions: <u>Epilogue</u>

*What will you most proudly remember
about your care-giving journey?*

Nourishment for Your Journey: Care-Giving Resources

I stated at the outset that this is not a book of answers—it is simply the story of one family's experience with memory loss and dementia in a loved one. I have also intentionally limited references to Alzheimer's disease. My mother was never diagnosed with that disease and there are many (over one hundred at last count) known causes for Alzheimer's-like symptoms, including dementia and memory loss, in an individual.

The saying goes, "If you know one person with Alzheimer's disease, you know, well, one person with Alzheimer's disease." The symptoms and behaviors associated with these various diseases of forgetting and dementia seen mostly in the aging vary so widely that any one experience of diagnosis, prognosis and care-giving should not be assumed to be typical. The hopeful aspect of this complexity is that research into medication, care-giving aids, effective communication skills, and life improvement therapies for the aging are constantly evolving.

Consequently, the single most important piece of advice I will offer to anyone caring for a loved one with Alzheimer's or other dementia disease is—get help! You may feel as though you are the only one responsible for your loved one's well-being, but you do not need to take on that task alone! Resources are available.

Your own general physician or medical care facility may be the best place to find a partner in seeking facts and solutions. Your local Social Services or Health and Human Resource Offices can also guide you toward answers and support. Both can point you toward invaluable resources for everything ranging from expert medical care, volunteer help with your loved one, solutions to financial and legal obstacles, services offering professional in-home and residential care options, and clinics or hospice-care providers specializing in elder care. For you, the caregiver, they will be able to suggest reading materials, support groups and respite care services.

Good places to start are, The Alzheimer's Foundation of America (www.alzfdn.org) or the Fisher Center for Alzheimer's Research Foundation (www.alzinfo.org).

Or search your local library for books. *Naomi Feil's Validation Therapy* offers one well-received approach to dealing with the unfamiliar perceptions and behaviors you may encounter with your loved one. For a new perspective on the diagnosis of Alzheimer's disease, consider *The Myth of Alzheimer's* by Peter J. Whitehouse.

You will see things among the resources that don't apply to your situation. But you will also find highly pragmatic solutions to the vexing problems you're facing daily, hints and ideas for coping, and the emotional support of feeling understood.

Whatever the details of your care-giving journey, I encourage you to honor your work and your loved one by not only giving good care, but also *taking* good care of yourself!

TRUE STORIES OF COURAGE AND INSPIRATION

> *Call in your order for fast service and quantity discounts!*
> **(541) 347- 9882**

OR order on-line at **www.rdrpublishers.com** *using PayPal.*
OR order by FAX at **(541) 347-9883** *OR by mail:*
Make a copy of this form; enclose payment information:

Robert D. Reed Publishers
1380 Face Rock Drive, Bandon, OR 97411

Name: _____

Address: _____

City: _____ State: _____ Zip: _____

Phone: _____ Fax: _____ Cell:_____

E-Mail:_____

Payment by check /_/ or credit card /_/ *(All major credit cards are accepted.)*

Name on card: _____

Card Number: _____

Exp. Date _____ Last 3-Digit number on back of card: _____

	Quantity	Total Amount

Travels in Place: A Journey into Memory Loss
by Christiane W. Griffin-Wehr .... $16.95 _____ _____

Fragments of a Forgotten People
by Henry Fast .... $15.95 _____ _____

Liberty's Quest: The Compelling Story of the Wife
and Mother of Two Poetry Pulitzer Prize Winners,
James Wright and Franz Wright
by Liberty Kovacs .... $29.95 _____ _____

The Quander Quality: The True Story of a Black
Trailblazing Diabetic
by James W. Quander
and Rohulamin Quander .... $24.95 _____ _____

Silent Screams from the Hamptons
by Christa Jan Ryan .... $15.95 _____ _____

Quantity of books ordered: _____Total amount for books: _____

Shipping is $3.50 1ˢᵗ book + $1 for each additional book.   Plus postage: _____

FINAL TOTAL: _____